JUST A WALK IN THE PARK

A Guide to Draft Dog Training

by

Barry Solomon

Copyright 2015 - All rights reserved

This book is dedicated to the "grandma's," Stacy Temples, Valerie Horney, and Dottie Schulte, the women with the sires and dams of all of my draft dogs. They entrusted some puppies to a raw beginner, and it turned out the dogs became pretty good at drafting. Stacy encouraged me to attend my first draft test to "see if it was something I might like to do."

Little did I know...

Photo Credits

Thanks to the following individuals for allowing the use of their photographs as the basis of my illustrations.

Barb LeTourneau
Inside front cover, Pgs. 34, 36, 42, 44 (top), 54, 62-70, 74-80, 86-90, 96, 104-160, 174-178, 186-202, 206-208, 216-218, 232

Ruth Nielsen
Pg. 0, Pg. 20 (Brace team), Pgs. 30, 92, 164, 166, 220

Jasen Duncan
Pg. 6 (Wagon), Pg. 8 (Locking Pin)

Alice Clark
Pg. 72

Models

Gandalf
CH Wagontales Great Grey Wizard
RN, NDD

Legend
CH Wagontale's Lady of the Lake
CGCA, CD, RAE, BN, NDD, BNDD, DD, BDD

Smokey
CH Wagontale's Sing Me a Miracle
CGC, CD, RE, GMDD, DD1, TDD1

Watson
CH Wagontale's Whodunnit?
CGC, CD, RE, GMDD, DD1, TDD1, NJC, WV-N, TN-N

Marshall
GCH Ebnets Hired Gun Frm Zanzbern
CD, GMDD, OJP, NFP, AXP

Acknowledgements

Michael Marks was not only the inspiration for this book, but also created the design, the 3d models, and all the illustrations. In the car, on the way home from a Draft Test in Minnesota, he asked, "Now that you have completed your second Grand Master Draft Dog title, what are you going to do next?" I suggested retirement, and he suggested this book. It looks like he got his way on this one.

Thanks to BMDCA Draft Judges Stacy Temples, Valerie Horney, and Ruth Nielsen for their technical review. Thanks to Ed Simstone for the review of the Newfoundland Draft test content, and to Michael Carr for the review of the Rottweiler test content. Finally, thanks to Candy McDanal for her proofreading expertise.

I would also like to thank my friend, Bob Tucker, for taking a few moments a long time ago at our club's "Working Dog Day" to show me how to harness and hitch my first dog. He then pointed forward and I've been drafting ever since.

Finally, I would like to thank my wife, Pam, who does most of the obedience and rally training, for creating future draft dogs that really know how to work. Most of our vacation time now includes heading from one draft test to the next, and I'm truly glad to have her support.

Disclaimer

The author is an Approved Bernese Mountain Dog Club of America Draft Judge, but is not a licensed nor professional dog trainer and makes no representations that the techniques discussed within this book are appropriate for all handlers or dogs. You know yourself and your dogs best, so train within the limits of yourself and your dogs. If the techniques recommended within this book do not seem to work for you, modify them, or consult with other experienced draft handlers before proceeding.

Table of Contents

Just a Walk in the Park	1
Equipment	7
Carts	7
Accessories and Options	15
Harnesses	21
Adjustments	29
Harness Adjustments	31
Cart Adjustments	43
Progression	61
Learn to Turn	75
Intangibles	85
Philosophy on Mindset	99
Basic Control	103
Walking under Control	113
Recall	115
Building on Turns, Halts, and Waits	123
Harness and Hitch	125
Weaves, Circles, 90-Degree Turns and About Turns	129
Halts and Waits	137
Distractions, Slows, Narrows, and Backs	153
Distractions	153
Slows	159
Narrows	163
Backs	173
Philosophy on Techniques	181
Group Exercises	187
Group Stay	193
Distance Freight Haul	201
Preparing for a Test	205
Philosophy on a Job Well Done	217
Alphabet Soup	221

Just a Walk in the Park

"Just a walk in the park," I once told my friend, Mike.

We had been discussing my role as a Draft Judge for the Bernese Mountain Dog Club of America (BMDCA), and he had asked what I looked for in a performance. How can you sum that up in only a few words, I wondered? How do you take huge concepts like baseball, or nuclear engineering, and distill them down to their very essence to explain them to someone who has never seen them before? Where to begin?

Bernese Mountain Dogs were originally bred in Switzerland as light draft animals for farms that often did not have horses or oxen. Berners traditionally pulled two-wheeled carts or four-wheeled wagons, and occasionally various sleds, travois, and toboggans depending upon the weather and terrain. Dairy farmers would haul full milk cans down to the local cheesery. Other uses included hauling logs and other farm materials. If they were lucky, small children could catch a ride in the cart. One, two, or more dogs could pull these carts, depending upon the load and configuration.

Parades are now popular activities, where groups of draft dogs pulling their carts are always greeted heartily. However, you will often find a similar reception while working with your dog in you own neighborhood or local park. Personally, I most enjoy drafting my dogs in place of their daily walk where I can get in twice the workout for them in half the distance when I add a little bit of a freight load to the cart.

In an effort to help keep these working instincts in the breed, the BMDCA, along with several other breed clubs, offers a standardized draft test that includes examples of the skills required for a dog to perform their traditional tasks. Exercises include harness and hitching, turns and circular patterns, slows, halts, backing, loading and unloading, working in constrained areas and around obstacles, working around visual and auditory distractions, stays, and all-terrain freight hauls. If you've never seen a draft test, you can think of it as a combination of obedience and obstacle course exercises, where the dog just happens to be hauling a cart.

And that gets me back to my original thought. What do I look for in a performance? Sure, there is a rulebook and there are specific parameters that describe passing and failing performances for each exercise, but many people who want to draft, do so without ever wishing to compete. Either way, if you read the "Purpose" paragraph printed inside the BMDCA rulebook cover, you can more fully understand the concept I'm getting at:

> "The Bernese Mountain Dog Club of America Draft Tests are a series of exercises designed to develop and demonstrate the natural abilities of purebred Bernese Mountain Dogs in a working capacity involving hauling. The Bernese Mountain Dog has historically functioned as a draft dog in various capacities, and performance of these exercises is intended to demonstrate skills resulting from both inherent ability and training which are applicable to realistic work situations. Efficiency in accomplishment of tasks is essential. It is also desirable that the dog evidence willingness and enjoyment of his work in a combination of controlled teamwork with his handler and natural independence."

In reading that I focus on these key words: willingness, enjoyment, and teamwork. I think back to all of the quiet times where it is just my dog and myself, alone on some wooded path. We're not going anywhere or doing anything with a particular goal in mind, but my dog is as happy to be there with me as I am to be there with him. Oh, and by the way, he just happens to be hauling his cart, with the autumn leaves crunching softly under the wheels.

And there it is – in competition or out, it's supposed to look the same. It's just a handler and their dog, performing one of the most enjoyable activities you can do together.

At its essence, it is "just a walk in the park," and on this late fall afternoon, that's what we're doing. Mike, his Bernese Mountain Dog, Shogun, myself, my Bernese Mountain Dog, Smokey, and his cart.

"I've seen you do it," said Mike, "and I understand exactly what you mean. You make it all look so effortless, and your dogs look like they will just stay on your heel wherever you lead them."

"They are good workers," I replied, "but make no mistake, this just doesn't happen overnight. Like anything else you can get really good at, you need to be willing to practice a lot and put in the time. Some breeds take to it far more easily than others, but that's just to get them pulling forward. Even Berners need to be taught how to turn, and slow, and back, and even to stop." I'm struck by the irony that only by working hard does something really ever look easy.

Mike pondered this for a few moments. "Well, I've never been afraid of a little bit of hard work. Shogun, he's going to be a bit of a handful, but I want to get there – 'just a walk in the park,' I mean. You wouldn't be willing to share some advice on how to get started, would you?"

"Certainly. The first thing we're going to need to do is get you some equipment. I'd recommend you borrow some of mine to try it out first. This can get a bit expensive and it's a good idea to know you and your dog are both willing and able before you commit. I've got a pretty good selection of harnesses and carts back home. Let's head over and we'll see if we can't find something to get you started."

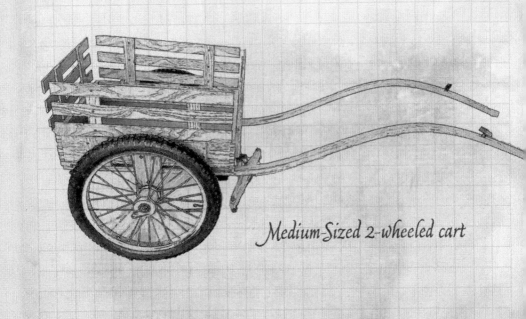

Medium-Sized 2-wheeled cart

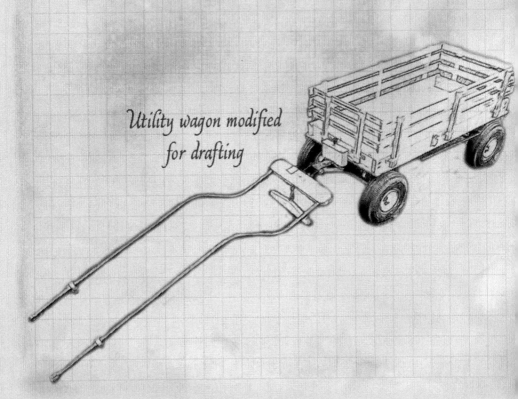

Utility wagon modified for drafting

Equipment

"Well, the concept is pretty simple," I told Mike later that day, "but the complexity is always in the details. Basically, all you need is a harness and something to pull. There are a few broad classifications of equipment that you need to be familiar with, and after that, there's a lot of theory-crafting and personal preference that comes into play.

"The first thing you will want to do is to pick what you are going to pull. Most people doing drafting, especially for competitions, will use a cart. A cart has two wheels which makes maneuvering pretty easy, but you will need to work to balance the freight load in the cart over the axle, because otherwise the weight forces the shafts upward or downward and neither is something you really want your dog to have to deal with. Typically you want the load directly over the axle; this makes it easier for the dog to control the weight. A lot of carts for both competition and utility purposes can be set up in this manner.

"If you really don't want to worry about the freight load, or you are planning on hauling lots of weight, than a wagon might be a better choice. Since a wagon has four wheels, you can pretty much put the load into the wagon any way you want, but the downside of four wheels is that you need the wagon to be able to steer, and than means that the front wheels need to be able to turn left and right.

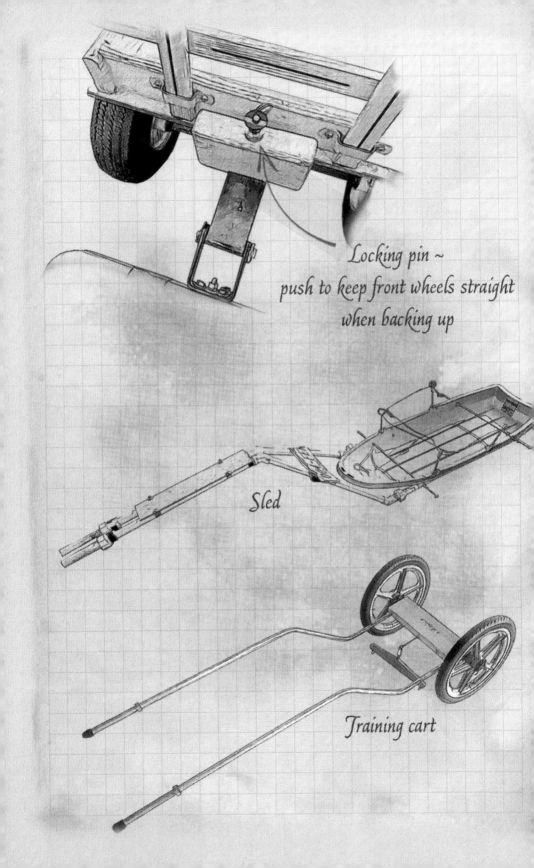

Locking pin ~ push to keep front wheels straight when backing up

Sled

Training cart

This adds a little complexity to the mechanism, but the real problem isn't so much going forward as it is going backwards. In order to back a wagon without it jackknifing, they typically have some sort of locking pin that will hold the front wheels centered for backing, but you need to remember to unlock afterwards otherwise you lose your steering. So even though competition typically requires a backing exercise, backing in general is one of your tools that you use for getting yourself out of bad alignments and tight spaces and a lot of people don't like the hassle of having to lock and unlock. I've only seen a few wagons used in competition, so people clearly seem to favor carts instead.

"Are there any other choices to consider," asked Mike.

"Depending upon terrain, and winter weather, you may also see people pulling sleds, toboggans, and travois. But if you thought wagons were problematic for backing, these can be outright impossible. And while a travois works in theory, it does provide a lot of drag and the angle makes it tough to retain a freight load, so you have to factor that into the equation as well. I think we can probably just consider these as novelties and you can focus on carts and wagons.

"Well it sounds like a cart is probably the way to go for my first purchase," said Mike. If I ever start building a collection I might think about a wagon at another time.

"OK, now that we've narrowed the focus down to carts, we still have many other things to consider. First and foremost is the size; without oversimplifying things, you basically have extra-small, small, medium, and large.

"In the extra-small category, I'd put training carts. Think about a small section of board set horizontally acting as an axle carrier with twelve inch wheels, and a couple of metal shafts. Functionally, this fills the role of the cart but provides the smallest possible size and weight profile. We often use these at our training camps for dogs that have never pulled before, for dogs that experience fear either being around a cart, or those that are especially suspicious of something 'following' them.

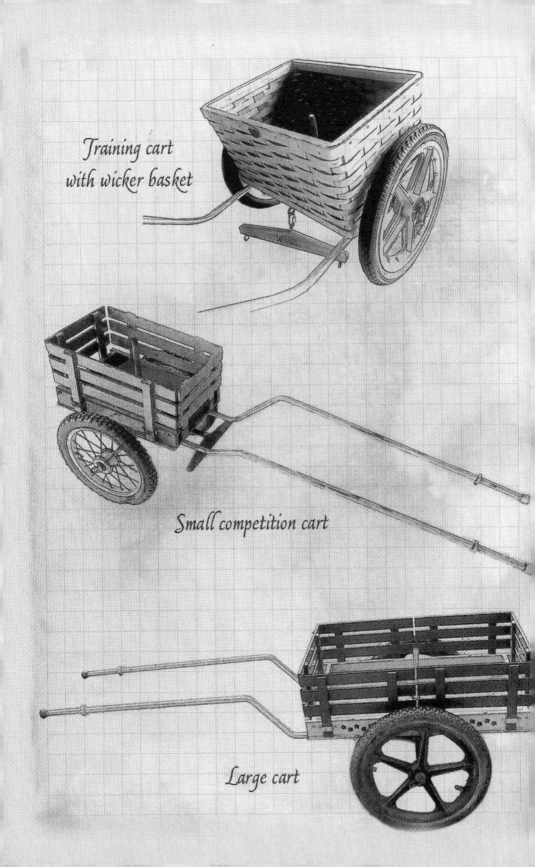

Training carts are the least expensive purchase you can make if you are worried that your dog may not take to drafting, and even these offer a few options that could get you into competitions. They often have the option to add a small wire or wicker basket to server as a cargo box, and this is sufficient to carry the twenty pounds of weight necessary for a novice-level freight haul. However, trying to add the freight load for an open-level freight haul is probably beyond the limits of the set-up. These training carts lend themselves to small dogs and smaller breeds in general, but you can also typically upgrade the wheels to sixteen inches which helps set the height of the shafts more correctly for larger dogs.

Also in the category of extra-small, there are some cart manufacturers that build carts specifically for small breeds, right on down to toy sizes. These aren't really a consideration for our large-breed dogs, but it's nice to know that there are manufacturers dedicated to the concept that you can teach virtually any breed to draft, so you need the right equipment available.

"In the small category, you will see what are known as 'competition' carts. That does not mean that other carts cannot be used for competition purposes, but it does highlight the fact that these small carts are typically not much good at anything other than competitions. Specifically, this size cart is meant to be extremely nimble with a very narrow axle width, and a cargo box sized just large enough to meet the needs of competition. Wheels size will vary from sixteen to twenty inches. They are very good for tight maneuvering purposes, but they don't provide much benefit for utility purposes. However, they are typically built with enough strength to carry an open-level freight haul weight load and enough adjustability to fit just about any dog. Unless someone has specific utility needs that would require a larger cart, most people will start with one of these competition carts.

"The medium and large carts are just larger variants that have larger cargo boxes and often the ability to haul more weight. If you want to carry little kids, or haul logs around your property, or do actual utility work around a farm, then a medium or large cart is probably what you want. They have wider axles to accommodate the larger cargo boxes, and this can make them a little less maneuverable; however, this is nothing you can't overcome when you train your

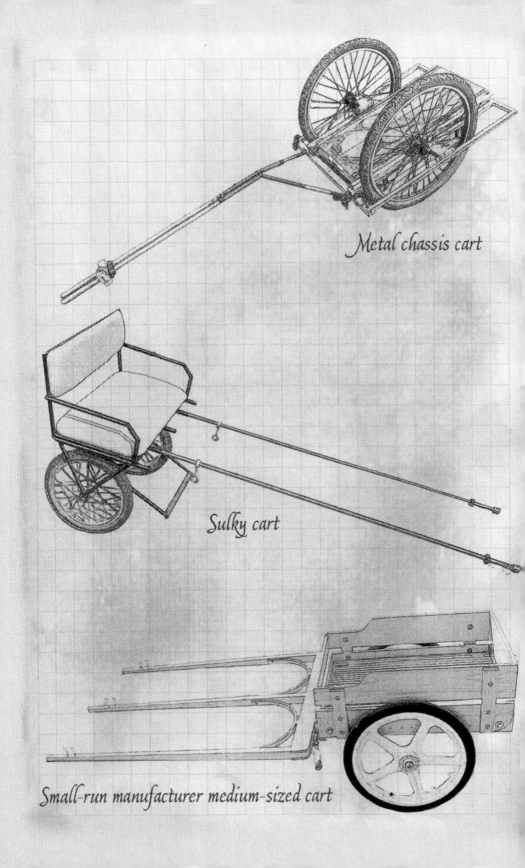

dog to turn. I'd say that I see a pretty good distribution of small, medium, and large carts all used for competition purposes, and they seem to get the job done.

In addition to the carts I've just described that are most typical in Berner competitions, you will also see some other types of carts that seem to be more popular with other breeds. At the Newfoundland tests I've been to, I've seen several all-metal carts that don't have axles per se, rather their wheels attach with quick-release bicycle-style hubs. Without the central axle, they can move their cargo boxes down considerably for a much lower center of gravity and they are certainly extremely durable. And for Rottweilers, their tests offer levels where the handler walks by the cart, much like the Berner and Newfie tests, but they also offer a level that includes 'driving' where the handler rides in the cart and controls the one or more dogs using reins rather than a leash.

Because of this, it's pretty typical to see sulky carts, which are built more around the concept of an elevated seat for the driver as opposed to a cargo box for carrying a separate freight load. These too can range from simple to complex with higher-end models having rather elaborate systems including active shock-absorbing suspensions and disc brakes. Bear in mind, for most carts the term 'brake' refers to a part of the shaft that anchors the harness to the cart.

"OK, what other considerations should I keep in mind when I decide to start shopping?"

"You have a couple of choices in where you get your cart. Some people make their own carts, either of their own design, or using plans they've found on the Internet. I've seen plain and fancy, in metal, wood, and PVC. I wouldn't necessarily recommend this route for your first cart, but if you do decide to make one, make sure it's substantial and 'locked-down.' I've seen some home-built carts shake themselves apart under load, and I've seen shafts rotate out of position, and wheels fall off.

"In addition to several commercial manufacturers you can find on the Web, there are also what I call small-run manufacturers. These are usually hobbyists who like woodworking and either have dogs or know people who participate in drafting. Often, for about the same price as a commercially made cart,

A typical competition freight load

Weights stacked over axle

they will make one of their design for you, and sometimes with you choice of woods and finishes. The difficulty here is that you pretty much need to find these guys through word-of-mouth because they usually don't advertise. The best way is often to go to a local draft competition and just check out the variety of carts available. Once you find something you like, the owner will often tell you where they got it.

"Other than that, I guess it's pretty similar to buying a car. I just described the basic models you can choose from, and then each model will have options for various trim levels and bells and whistles, all of which can affect the price, flexibility and aesthetics of the cart, but functionally, they are all pretty much the same. In general, you will want to look at a few key areas and determine what you can and can't live with. Here's a few of the things I look for.

"For the cargo box, I like a shallow box with taller, light-weight side panels that can be removed. This offers flexibility to vary the cart depending upon the load. In many cases, items are lightweight and bulky, so the side panels can keep them contained within. They should remove easily to allow me to tear down the cart for transport, but they should not fall out easily or should allow for some way to positively attach them to the cart because you don't want pieces falling off if you hit a bump. I like the slats to be pretty close together so that nothing accidentally falls out. I also look for attachment points where I can hook on bungee cords or a small cargo net to help retain a freight load if necessary.

"Of course, the main purpose of the cargo box is to hold the freight load. For lightweight items, you can just toss them into the cart and let the sides of the box retain the items. If you are going to be hauling a practical freight load, such as logs or a milk canister, it will be up to you as the handler to ensure that the load is balanced so that the shafts do not apply an upward or downward force on your dog's back. This can take several iterations of loading to get everything set up and balanced correctly. If you are doing training or competitions, many people prefer a weight insert for the cargo box that ensures that the freight load is centered over the axle. These inserts are set up to accept a stack of barbell weights and make loading and balancing quick and easy.

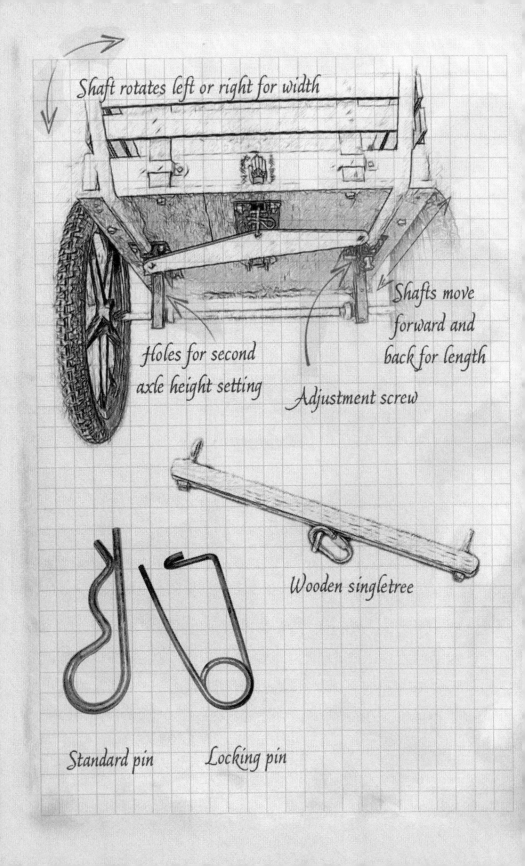

"For the undercarriage, both metal and wood can work equally well. Look for adjustability most of all. Does the cart allow me to change the height? I prefer at least two height settings for the axle as this allows me to adjust for dogs of different height. Does the cart allow me to change the shaft length and shaft width? Some don't which can be limiting, and some do with various degrees of ease.

These are not things you tend to change often, but if you have multiple dogs of differing sizes, these adjustments can help a lot. Additionally, determine what mechanism is in place for the attachment of the traces from the harness to the cart. Many carts offer singletrees, which allow a degree of rotation from side to side to help smooth out the pulling motion the dog transfers to the cart. If there are singletrees, they should be removable, and preferably they do not be attached in a way that lets them bang into the shafts as this causes a lot of noise.

"As to the axle, it should be set up to allow the wheels to be removed easily for teardown purposes. If it has removable pins holding the wheels on, you might want to consider upgrading these to locking pins since the removable ones tend to fall out. If the axle is a standard size, determine if there are options for different sized wheels, as these can also help adjust the height of the cart for different dogs.

"Carts typically come with wheels and tires included. In general, there is not a wide variety of cart wheels available for purchase on the Internet, so you usually have to stick to whatever the manufacturer has available. Sometimes they offer options or upgrades, so here are a few things to consider. First, there are a couple of different diameter axles that are commonly used, with ½" and 5/8" being the most common. A smaller diameter axle is lighter in weight but can't support as much load as a larger diameter."

"Most cart wheels utilize bearings that press into the wheel hubs, so while it is often possible to change bearings to move wheels between different axle diameters, it is usually better to just verify that axle diameter and wheel bearing match before you purchase."

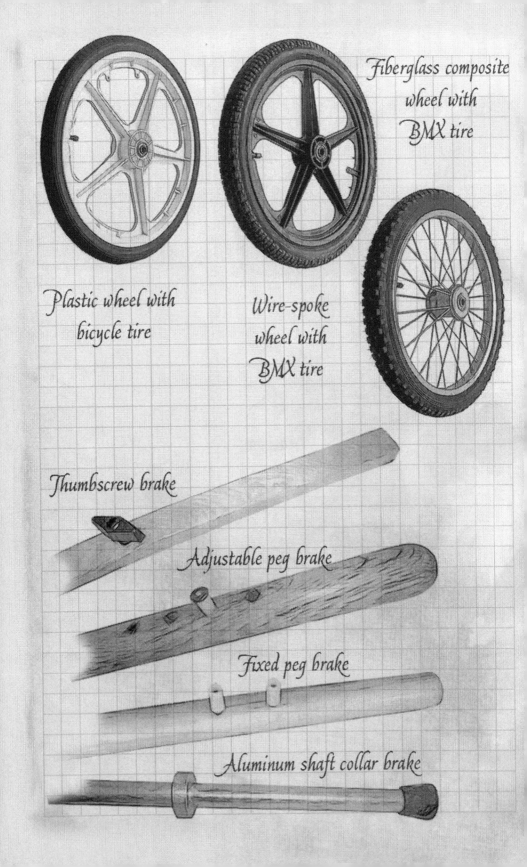

"Next, cart wheels are made from different materials, including plastic, fiberglass composite, metal-spoke, and occasionally even wooden-spoke. Some of this equates to personal preference in the aesthetics of the wheel, but bear in mind that plastic wheels are usually the least sturdy, and can distort under heavy loads – fiberglass and metal-spoke can be better choices if you are planning on hauling a lot of weight. Most wheels offer pneumatic tires with inner tubes, although it is also possible to get solid rubber tires or even steel-rimmed wooden wheels with no tires. The pneumatic tires offer the best flexibility, but you do need to remember that you can draft across thorns or other items that can cause leaks and flats in your inner tubes, so consider upgrading them to puncture-resistant or self-sealing varieties. Solid rubber avoids these problems, but they tend to dig into the ground a bit. Finally, you may have a choice of traditional bicycle tires or BMX style knobby tires. Again this is mostly an aesthetic choice, although the BMX tires tend to be wider which helps somewhat with weight distribution on softer surfaces, as well as providing a bit more tread which can help prevent your cart from sliding if you are traversing across the face of a hill rather than perpendicular to it."

"For the shafts, you will want to look at the braking mechanisms provided and they should offer a degree of adjustment forward and back along the shafts. Also, consider how quickly and easily the shaft can be removed for teardown. Most carts with aluminum shafts have angles bent into them allowing for them to be attached low on the cart, which can be more efficient, but you probably don't want to talk about moment arms and center of gravity.

Most carts with wooden shafts have straight shafts because they are easier to produce, and they tend to attach higher up the sides of cart. Some wooden carts have options for bent wooden shafts, which do attach lower like the aluminum bent shaft carts. Mostly the differences are aesthetic, but there may be some additional value to the curved wooden shafts as the shaft tips pass downwards once they pass through the shaft rings on the harness. This keeps the tips lower and outside of the dog's peripheral vision which could help for a dog that doesn't like the shafts bouncing up around their head.

"I know that sometimes you work with both your dogs at the same time," said Mike. "Does that take a special cart set-up?"

"That's called 'a brace' when you work two dogs together side-by-side. There are various ways to accomplish this, but for the most part, you need a way to have three shafts so that each dog has one on both their left and right sides. Several of the manufacturers sell conversion kits that let you add a center shaft and either move or rotate the other shafts out wider. Another way to do this is by using a replaceable yoke assembly that uses the existing two shaft mounting locations. You remove the single shafts and replace them with the yoke assembly to have brace shafts. This can be convenient for travel and teardown if you have enough space to store everything in a single assembly. After a while, you may find that it gets tiresome converting a single cart back and forth, so that's the time many people end up buying their second cart, which will typically be larger than their first and with a brace set up option.

As you can imagine, there's no one perfect cart for all of the jobs you can perform with them, so you end up picking the one with the best set of features to meet most of your needs. Here's a list of some of the manufacturer's you'll find on the Web."

"Next, we'll switch our attention to harnesses. There are two main styles to choose from, and after that, it's pretty much the sky's the limit in terms of materials, colors, and features.

"The more 'traditional' style is called a parade or chest harness. These are sort of scaled-down models of horse tack. They are nice because they look old-school, they are relatively uncomplicated, and are easy to get on and off your dog as they just slip on over the dog's head and single strap run under the dog's belly to a buckle is often all there is too it. In fact, you will sometimes see the harnesses left fully attached to the cart, and you simply tilt the shafts and harness over the dog's head, lower it down, and buckle, and you're ready to draft."

"That sounds easy enough, but you said there are two styles of harnesses, so I suspect your going to tell me there's a down-side to these as well."

"That's a pretty good guess on your part. The issue most people have with these parade harnesses is the fact that they pass horizontally across the dog's chest at a height of their upper arms. That means they have a tendency to restrict the dog's movement in the front and they can't reach out as far to pull.

This becomes especially problematic when the cart is under a freight load as the more the cart resists the pull forward, the tighter the pull of the harness across the chest and the more restrictive it becomes. Some people will use these harnesses for novice level competition where freight load is really not much of a consideration, or for parades and such as the name implies. If you are really going to pull any weight, most people will switch to or just start out with a Siwash harness."

"Siwash harnesses are based around a fitted 'collar' that goes around the dog's head, but it has a vertical strap that extends down under the dog's chest and between their front legs. This means that the weight load is distributed along the dog's chest, but without the restriction in movement that I described for the parade harnesses.

The difficulty with a Siwash harness is that you have a lot of straps and essentially a left side and right side that need to extend out along the dog's sides. Because of the vertical design along the chest, the only way to get this harness on the dog is to lift the dog's front legs, one at a time, to step over the side straps to allow the chest piece to get underneath the dog. So what you gain in the overall effectiveness of the harness, you lose to added complexity of getting it on the dog in the first place. Luckily, once you learn to do this, it's not that hard to do, and we sometimes train this exercise blindfolded, so it's really not as bad as it sounds. Overall, I'd say Siwash harnesses far outnumber parade harnesses in competition."

"Well, I like the idea of not outgrowing the harness in terms of being able to handle weight at some point in the future, so I'm leaning towards Siwash myself. What else do we need to look for?"

"Both styles of harnesses will have some sort of 'shaft ring' that allows the cart shafts to slide through to essentially hold the harness in a fixed position relative to the cart. Both styles will also have some sort of 'trace attachments,' which are typically small metal rings that allow the 'traces' to attach between the harness and the cart. The 'traces' are typically straps with buckles or clips for easy attachment and removal that function to allow the dog's harness to pull the cart forward. The harness and traces are usually included together for a single price, but either way, make sure you get both a harness and traces.

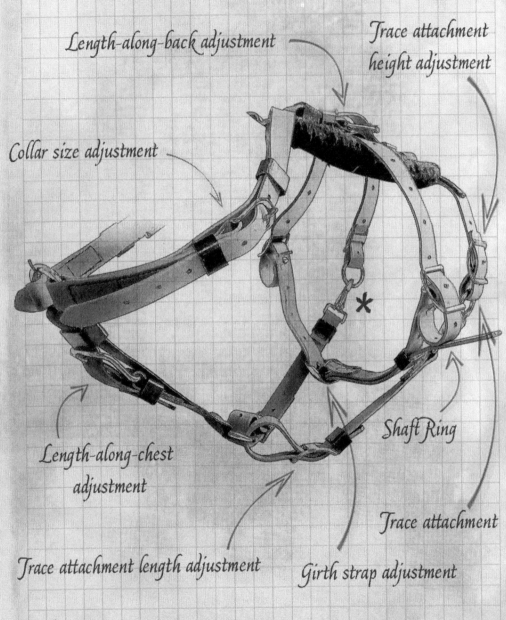

"The rest of your choices are based around flexibility, cosmetics, and price. For flexibility, look for the harness to have multiple adjustment, especially around size and positioning of the shaft rings around the girth strap, and for adjusting the height and length of the trace attachments. Many of the basic Siwash harnesses are based upon a fixed 'collar' size, so you must measure and pick the harness specifically for a particular dog.

Some of the higher-end harnesses allow for adjustments in the 'collar' portion, length along the chest, and length along the back, which are all nice if you have a younger dog that is still growing into their body, or if you have multiple dogs who will be sharing a harness. Keep in mind that even the high-end harnesses are not infinitely adjustable, but rather are based upon you taking a few key measurements for your dog, and then the adjustability is built around those measurements. Figure to spend significantly more for a harness with these types of adjustments.

I will tell you that adjusting these harnesses is not the most convenient thing, so the reality is that if you are worrying about multiple dogs, it's probably better to spend the extra money on additional harnesses as otherwise you find yourself constantly readjusting rather than spending time practicing.

"Most harnesses are available in multiple colors, and some offer you a choice of a base color with an accent color. Some harnesses include padding, especially across the tops of the shoulders and along the chest, which is often removable so you can wash them separately from the harness. Basic Siwash harnesses are made from nylon webbing, but you can also upgrade to leather or Biothane, which can make the harness look and feel more substantial, but also increases the weight. I really like my Biothane harnesses but many people comment as to how heavy they are. I'm fond of saying that if your dog has difficulty carrying the weight of their harness, you have other issues you need to deal with before you hook them up to the cart."

"I do see that your Biothane harnesses are very adjustable, but I also see what appears to be an extra set of buckles along the side," said Mike. "What is the purpose of those?"

DOG WORKS
(WWW.DOGWORKS.COM)

WILCZEK WOODWORKS
(WWW.WILCZEKWOODWORKS.COM)

EMBELLISHED LAMB
(WWW.EMBELLISHEDLAMB.COM)

NORDKYN OUTFITTERS
(WWW.NORDKYN.COM)

"Ah, you have good eyes. This harness is called a 'modified Siwash.' You recall we talked about having to lift the dog's feet to step into a Siwash. This particular harness allows me to unclip the side straps, so basically I just lift the collar portion over my dog's head, and then without lifting his paws, I can reach under his chest and clip first one side and then the other. This makes this harness much easier to get on and off than other Siwash harnesses.

"As much as I like and would recommend these harnesses, they are a bit pricey, especially for an entry-level harness, so I would suggest you start with a basic nylon Swiash, and once you know that you do and don't like about it, you can keep that in mind when you buy your next harness. You are welcome to try out all of these, and you can borrow one if you like. When you think you're ready to buy, here's a list of harness manufacturers you can find on the Web."

"I noticed that you have matching collars to your harnesses," said Mike. I didn't picture you or your dogs as being so fashion-conscious."

"Some people do think it does look nice to have the dog's collar and harness match for purely cosmetic reasons. You'll see this often in brace because two different dogs will have two differently adjusted harnesses, and color-coding a harness to a collar is one way to keep this straight under stress. But color-coordinated or not, I do recommend that you get a special collar that you only use for drafting.

"There is no such thing as a 'drafting collar' and you are not looking for any special features, but keep in mind that electronic training collars and pinch or prong collars are generally prohibited. The purpose for this collar, especially in training, is to help get your dog into a working mindset. When you draft, you use the special collar, and you only use it to draft. Removing their usual collar, and putting on their drafting collar should be accompanied by something you repeat, like, 'OK, it's time to work!' or 'Let's go drafting!' or whatever else you want to use.

"Getting them out of their harness and collar at the end of a session is also a good time to remind them that they are a very hard worker and they deserve a big treat. And that doesn't need to be food. You can give them their favorite toy, or as you'll see with my boys, this is the time they get to jump up and give me a hug."

Adjustments

A couple of weeks later, Mike pulled his truck up to my house with a surprise. Apparently, our overview session on drafting equipment inspired him to go out and make an initial purchase: a basic nylon Siwash harness, and a wooden Competition Cart with aluminum shafts. This really wasn't too astonishing – Mike tends to be an "all-in" kind of guy, and after all, I had bought the same set of equipment several years back for my first draft dog.

"Mike," I said, "one of the most difficult parts of drafting happens before your dog ever pulls their cart. Since you are new to the concept, and have just bought or borrowed your first harness and cart, you will be faced with what seems to be an infinite supply of buckles, straps, and parts whose names you do not know, all of which need to be set-up specifically for your dog. Have no fear! We'll get you through it all, with plenty of tips and tricks along the way.

"The first step is to resist the urge to dive in right away. Even when you have an experienced mentor you're working with, don't expect to do anything more than some basic adjustments on the harness itself. Often, the first fitting of the harness to the dog can be accomplished in a comfortable environment, such as your living room, and the cart does not need to be present. You will have plenty of time later to bring the cart adjustments into the equation, but for now, keep it simple for both your dog and yourself.

"The second step is to remember that everything you are about to work through will be iterative in nature. The more familiar you become with your harness an cart, how it fits your dog, and how all of the parts work together as

a system, the more likely it is that you realize that your first set of adjustments needs to be tweaked somewhat. Even experienced handlers can have difficulty getting their harness and cart properly adjusted. Often it takes another set of eyes watching you work your dog under a variety of conditions to notice something subtle that could be improved. If you don't have that second set of eyes available to you, the adjustment procedure you work through here will get you dialed in over time."

"Keep in mind that proper adjustments of the harness to the dog and to the cart are crucial for you eventual success as a team. If you are somewhat off in your adjustments, this could results in some sloppiness in the overall system, making your team not perform as efficiently as possible. In more extreme cases, improper adjustments can result in your dog becoming unwilling to perform basic maneuvers, such as turns, halts, or pulling weight in the cart. Exceptionally improper set-up can lead to potential safety issues, which could result in your dog being injured, or overturning their cart.

"If you have the opportunity, work with another handler or an assistant as you work through your adjustments. If you have the opportunity to attend a local 'Working Dog' demonstration on drafting or a Draft Camp, these are both excellent ways to accelerate your progress. And remember to treat, treat, treat, and treat again! Have plenty of treats available for the harness adjustment session. Although you will be just asking your dog to essentially remain stationary, you may be surprised how time consuming an initial sizing session can be. Try to keep your sessions short, and always end on a positive note."

"The next thing you need to recognize is that you have numerous options for harnesses. Some have multiple adjustments, and others have certain settings fixed and so you knew that must order your harness to fit Shogun. Even highly adjustable harnesses are often built around your specific dog by setting the expected adjustments for your dog at the center of the adjustment range. I expect that you followed the sizing and measuring instructions from the manufacturer's Web site before ordering."

"Absolutely," said Mike. "I now know that one of the most important measurements is the sizing of the 'collar' portion of a Siwash harness, especially since this is non-adjustable on the harness I just purchased.

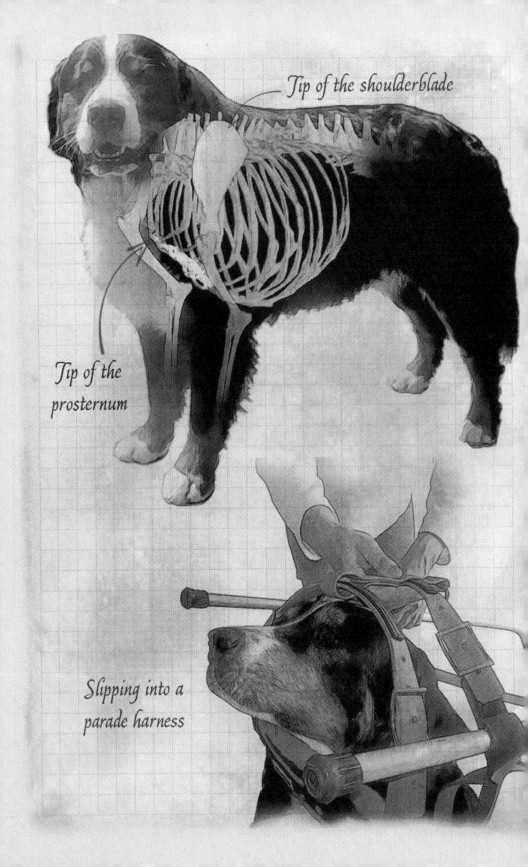

Tip of the shoulderblade

Tip of the prosternum

Slipping into a parade harness

The 'collar' measurement occurs from the withers just between the tips of the shoulder blades, down to the tip of the prosternum. I measured this around the neck on each side of my dog until both measurements were in agreement, then doubled the number to get the total Siwash collar size."

Mike continued, "So when we reviewed the equipment, you told me that most Bernese Mountain Dogs fall in the range of 24" to 30". Shogun fell into this size range. Since I was buying just a basic nylon Siwash harness, this was the only measurement I really needed. I expect that if I ever decide to step up to a custom harness, I'll be asked for several various length and girth measurements as well."

For comparison purposes, I pulled out one of my parade harnesses. I told Mike that, "Parade or chest style harnesses have larger openings that fit more easily over a dog's head, but the same withers to sternum measurement is used to size the harness. When placed over the dog's head, either a Siwash or Parade harness should sit atop the dog's shoulder blades and should have the "chest plate" resting across the sternum. Harnesses with collar sizes too small or too large will be uncomfortable for the dog and will not allow you to meet both of these positioning requirements.

I then took out one of my custom-made Siwash harnesses. "If you have an adjustable harness collar, use the buckle adjustments to set the collar size as we just discussed."

"Our first step," I said, "is to get the dog into the harness. Before we start working with your new Siwash, let me show you why some people still like to use parade or chest harnesses. As you can see, this harness slips very easily over the dog's head. All you need to do is pull backwards on the trace attachments and run them along the dog's sides to ensure that nothing is tangled or twisted. Then you run the girth strap around the dog's rib cage and outside of any other parts of the harness and buckle it into position. The girth strap should be tightened to the point that you are just able to slip your hand underneath it. Basically, I can get a dog into an already adjusted parade harness in a couple of seconds by just attaching one buckle. But we already discussed why I prefer Siwash harnesses, and since you bought one, let's go ahead and start working with that now.

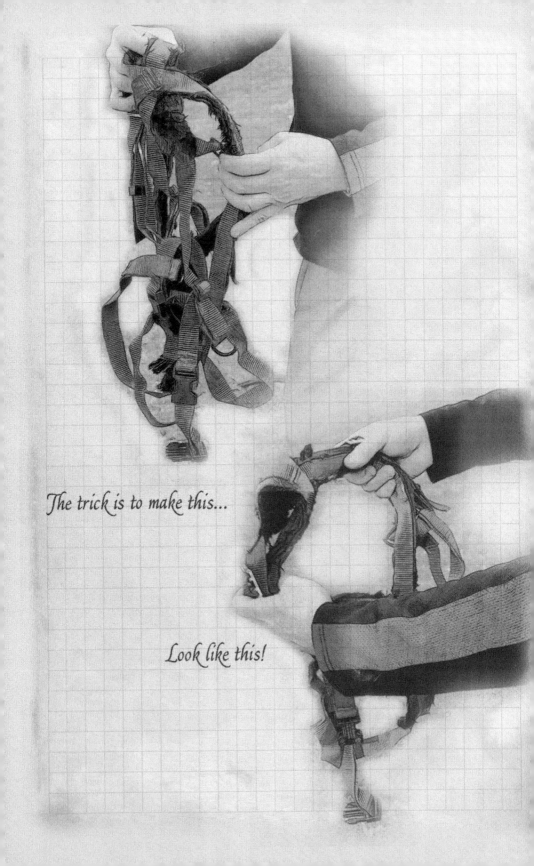

"First things first. Some Siwash harnesses have girth straps and belly bands that are completely removable from the rest of the harness. Until you are more familiar with getting this harness onto your dog, I suggest that you remove these straps and set them aside for the time being.

"Arrange the harness so that it is not tangled and gently gather all of the left side straps into your left hand and then grab the left side of the collar portion of the harness. Gather the right side straps and then grab the right side of the collar portion of the harness. In this way, you can create a short "tube" that you can look through that will easily slip over Shogun's head.

"Slip the harness over his head and gently pull the trace attachments back along the dog's sides. Now locate a portion of strap extending from the bottom of the chest piece and along to the trace attachment on one side of your dog. This strap needs to pass between his front legs and re-emerge on the side behind the front leg. In order to do this, you will gently need to lift his paw, and pull it up high enough for the strap to settle underneath the leg. Once you have done this, lower his paw and again pull gently on the trace attachment to extend it along the side of the dog. Move around and repeat this process on the other side. Ensure that the chest piece is centered and resting on the sternum, then extends between the front legs without any twists or tangles.

"Some dogs can get a little fussy when you lift their front paws. Like any other aspect of training your dog, work to get the behavior you want, treat frequently, and once you get the behavior, you can add a word to it. I taught my dogs the command 'lift' and I use it whenever I have to raise their front paws.

"Alright, now that everything is in the position I described, run the girth strap around his rib cage, and attach it using the buckles provided. The girth strap should be tightened to the point that you are just able to slip your hand underneath it. Once you are more familiar with getting a Siwash harness over your dog's head and between his front legs, you can keep the girth strap partially attached and fold this into the "tube" as well as you are arranging the harness.

"Some Siwash harnesses incorporate a belly band. This is an additional strap that adds some 'structural integrity' to the harness by keeping the trace attachments tight along the side of the dog. Once you are more experienced or are planning on doing a lot of weight pulling, I would recommend using this strap. Since you are a beginner, a belly band becomes just one more point of complication, so I recommend that you set it aside for the time being, and start using it later as you become more familiar with the rest of the harness.

"For now, just so you see it put on properly, when you are using a belly band, weave it through the attachment points provided and buckle it underneath your dog's belly. It should be tightened to the point that you are just able to slip your hand underneath it.

"In all cases, I recommend that you have the girth strap as the innermost strap and closest to the dog, running it beneath of any other pieces of the harness. Under load, the trace attachment straps will become taught to the body of the dog which will in turn help keep the girth strap and more importantly the shaft rings in the proper position which makes for a more consistent pulling experience for your dog.

Mike looked a little puzzled. "What would happen if the girth strap was run over the top of everything else – would it really be that bad?"

"Well, in most cases, you might not even notice it, especially with little or no weight in the cart. But in some cases, especially when the shafts are set a bit wide, you can see the shaft rings on the harness trying to pull the girth strap away from the body of the dog. This can set up sort of a 'trampoline' effect and you'll see the shafts start to bounce in rhythm with the dog's steps.

"Also, some judges scrutinize the harness more so than others, so you may as well start by learning to get this right to begin with.

"Next, since your harness has adjustments for the length and height of the trace attachments, let's begin to adjust these now. Ideally the trace attachment rings will sit on top of the rear part of the dog's rib cage. This keeps the harness from digging into the dog's belly and keeps them far enough forward to ensure free movement of the dog's thighs between the traces.

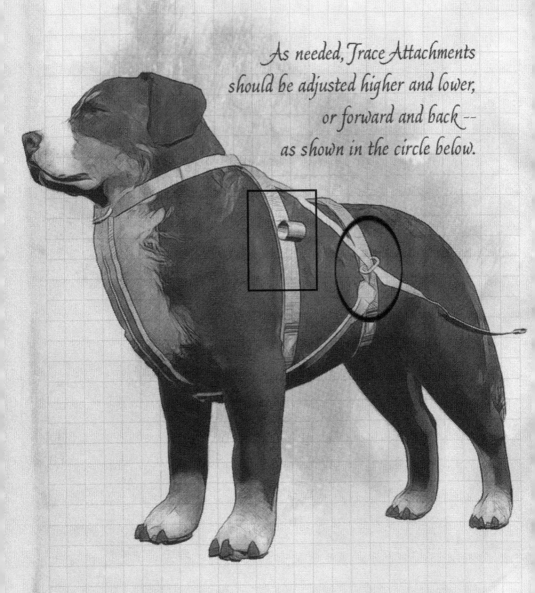

"It is hard to describe "too low" or "too high" as the angle of the traces will vary based upon the attachment point to your particular cart. The trace attachments should be on the "side" of the dog, as opposed to beneath the belly, or up on the back. Suffice it to say that when properly adjusted, the dog should have a good free range of motion in his rear and should not be constricted by the trace attachments in any way."

"If I happened to have a harness without these adjustments, " Mike asked, "what would I do?"

"Well, if you felt your dog's natural movement was constricted, then I would recommend that it would be a good time to try a different harness, or depending upon your sewing skills, to add some adjustability into the harness. Luckily, you won't have to worry about this.

"Next up, we'll need to set the shaft rings. The shaft rings sit on the girth strap and are used to attach the harness to the shafts of the cart. The shaft rings primarily allow for the cart to be steered by the dog, and support the braking function that allows the dog to stop the cart from moving forwards, or allows the dog to move the cart backwards in conjunction with the brakes. Depending upon the harness, the shaft rings can be adjusted somewhat independently of the girth strap or may require you to completely readjust the girth strap itself each time you reposition the shaft rings. This adjustment can often require multiple changes to get correct. I would say, this is probably the most difficult set of harness adjustments to get correct because several things have to get adjusted in unison, all of which will result in the shaft rings being in the correct location and the girth strap being re-sized correctly.

"The shaft ring itself must be sized to be just larger than the diameter of the shaft, allowing it to slide back to make contact with the brake, but it must not be so large that it can slide over the brake. Let's take a quick look at the size of the shafts on the cart to make sure we get this set correctly.

"Unless you have an extremely patient dog, you may want to take the harness or at least the girth strap, if removable, completely off the dog while you work on your adjustments.

"For a reference location, let's find the forward 'point' of the shoulder for Shogun. The center of the shaft from your cart should run across the point of your dog's shoulder to ensure a solid surface and maximum comfort for your dog when applying pressure in turns."

Mike asked, "What if your cart's shafts won't naturally cross the dog's shoulder at this 'point' location. Wouldn't we just adjust the shaft rings to a different location?"

"No," I said, "That's not a harness adjustment. Getting the shaft across the shoulder at the correct location is extremely critical as it can affect the dog's ability and willingness to turn. We'll discuss how to correct this when we go through cart adjustments.

"Let's adjust the position of the shaft rings relative to the girth strap so that the center of the shaft rings is just slightly above the point of the shoulder. This assumes that once the cart's shafts are in position, the slight weight of the shafts will pull the harness down somewhat. Once the shaft rings are positioned properly on each side, readjust the girth strap buckles to loosen or tighten until you can just slip your hand beneath the girth strap.

"Now that we have your harness properly adjusted, let's see if Shogun is still willing to work for you. Remove and replace the harness a couple of times to make sure you are fully familiar with the procedure. If he's done cooperating for now, let's just remove the harness, and plan another short session at a later time where you can continue working to make your dog comfortable with the harness. Adjusting the cart will take us some time and we want to make sure he's ready for that before we begin.

"It looks like he's relatively comfortable being in the harness. You can continue to build familiarity with the harness by putting it on him as he relaxes around the house. Some dogs don't have any concerns with the harness itself, so you may be able to proceed through this exercise very quickly. Otherwise, use multiple short sessions, treat frequently, and always end on a good note.

"Next up, we'll want to work through some cart adjustments, but before we do that, let's see how Shogun reacts to being near the cart itself. Depending on what we see, we'll either be able to move forward relatively quickly, or you may have some homework to do before we can proceed. Let's just put the cart down on the driveway, and then you leash walk him around it a few times.

Mike said, "What exactly are you looking for?"

"I'm trying to see if he is in any way leery of the cart. Some dogs will not show any fear around the cart, and some are not quite as certain of it. If you can get him to approach it a few times, and preferably step over and across the shafts, we're in business. Of course, you'll be treating him through this, so be generous and reward him frequently as he gets near.

"So far, so good. Since the cart doesn't frighten him, we can up the difficulty a little bit. If he wouldn't approach it at all, you would have your first homework assignment. You would need to continue to treat him around the proximity of the cart until he's comfortable being around it. Some people actually bring the cart indoors and work in their living rooms where it's a bit more relaxed and with far fewer distractions. I know people who go so far as to serve their dog's dinner with the bowl placed between the shafts or in the cargo box of the cart.

"In our case, I'll want you to just leash walk him around the driveway, and I'll walk with the cart. We'll vary how far apart we are, and ideally, he'll let me walk with it next to and behind him. If everything goes really well, I might nudge him a couple of times with the shafts to see if he reacts. You'll treat him each time I approach him with the cart. Since he's been around my dogs while they pull their carts, I'm hoping that this will proceed smoothly and quickly. Otherwise…

"Yeah, I know," said Mike, "more homework. I'm starting to sense a pattern here."

"They say you can teach almost any dog to draft. There are multiple steps, and we've already worked through a couple of them. Getting the dog in the harness and willing to work near the cart can range from a few seconds to a few weeks worth of work, depending on the breed and the individual dog. Berners

tend to get through these steps very quickly, so I'm not too surprised to see this move right along.

After a few minutes, we're both pleasantly surprised at our progress and we're ready for the next step. "Alright, let's see if we can get him to stand in between the shafts. I prefer to have the dog stand with you treating him, and I'll slowly bring the cart into position from behind. Later, you can choose to continue this method which many people use, eventually without the treats, or you can teach him how to approach the cart and step into the shafts himself. For now, since our goal is the first round of cart adjustments, let's just get him to stand comfortably between the shafts.

"Much like your harness, you may have few or many adjustments you can make, depending upon the style of cart and manufacturer. Since this is the first time you are bringing a beginner dog, a new harness, and a new cart together, you need to be willing to settle for 'good enough'. You will have plenty of time to fine-tune your adjustments in future sessions. Avoid the temptation of making too many tweaks all at the same time, especially without moving the dog and cart to see how everything fits together with a bit of drag pulling the cart back. Also avoid making your Shogun stand in position too long while you work through multiple adjustments as he will just get bored and at this point will not understand why you are asking him to stand still. As always, treats are your friend as you work through the cart adjustments.

"Since your cart allows you to adjust the length of the shafts, let's set them long enough so as to allow them to protrude in front of the points of the shoulders by 2-3 inches."

Mike asked, "What's the significance of them protruding in front by that exact amount?"

"Well, the 2-3 inches in front of the point of the shoulder allows enough shaft length so that the dog's shoulder can turn the cart. Too short allows the tips of the shafts to move back behind the upper arm if the cart is under load. Too long allows the shafts to stick out in front of the dog where the dog may see them in their peripheral vision. You can imagine, that would be distracting! If your dog pulls happily but refuses to turn, this adjustment is a likely source of the problem.

"With the shafts in position in front of the shoulder, there should be enough room that the dogs rear feet can stride backwards without kicking up against the front of the cart, or against any single or doubletree device the cart may include. As you can see, this adjustment is difficult to accomplish without moving the dog and cart and getting a good visual on the position of the dog's rear feet as they are moving, so approximate it for now, and plan to fine tune later. If you find yourself with "extra" shaft length once you have set the position relative to the point of the shoulders, meaning there is now a lot of distance between the rear of the dog and the front of the cart, you can either leave this as is or adjust the shafts backwards now.

"What is the disadvantage of having the shafts too long?"

"The further forward the dog is relative to the cart, the longer the turning radius will be, so ultimately your turns will not be as tight and precise. However, if you have multiple dogs of different sizes, you will either want to adjust the shafts for the longest dog and leave them, or set different "marks" for each dog and adjust for each dog accordingly. Depending upon the ease of this adjustment, most people will just pick one shaft length and leave it. For now, even if they are a little long, this should be fine for your initial training sessions.

"If you really wish to adjust the shafts backwards, we can do that now, but let's make sure we're not keeping Shogun waiting while we do so. Let's let him go play, or crate him while we work. Since this might take a while, I even recommend that you remove his harness so that he will start gaining awareness that putting the harness on means that cart pulling will commence immediately.

"Depending upon the method of adjustment, shortening the shafts relative to the cart can result in the rear of the shafts protruding back behind the cart."

"Is that a problem?"

"This is not preferable for both aesthetic and practical reasons as they can snag objects you are turning around. At this point we would mark and then remove the shafts to actually shorten them with a saw. Bear in mind, that doing so may limit you for different dogs in the future, but many cart manufacturers sell replacement shafts and having two sets may be required if your dogs are very different in size.

"If you happened to have a cart where you cannot adjust your shafts rearward, and if the dog's rear relative to the cart front appears to be correct, and the shaft tips are protruding 6" or more in front of the points of the shoulder, then that would likely the time to shorten the tips of the shafts with a saw.

"Why would you want to shorten the tips like that?"

"Well, too much extra shaft length in front of the point of the shoulders can create safety issues as the shaft tips encroach along the side of the dog's head. Depending upon load, the shaft tips can appear in the dog's peripheral vision or actually bump underneath or along the side of the dog's head. Either of these occurrences will make your dog reluctant to pull the cart.

"If your cart does not allow shaft length adjustments, work first on the positioning of the tips relative to the shoulder and always leave the extra length between the rear of the dog and the front of the cart. If the shafts are just too short to meet the adjustments as I've described, you will need to find a different cart for your dog, or possibly move the attachment point of the singletree rearwards underneath the cart so that the dogs rear feet move free and clear.

"Now that we have the shaft length correct, ideally, the shafts should be parallel to the ground when held in place by the shaft rings on your dog's harness. While it might not be possible to meet the ideal, as long as we don't deviate too far from parallel, there are usually no issues.

"We discussed this adjustment while working on the position of the shaft rings. If the shafts are angled extremely upwards, this can put the tips of the shafts up near your dog's head and can result in reluctance to pull the cart at all. If the shafts are angled extremely downwards, this can shift more of the weight load into a downwards force on your dog's back, resulting in reluctance to pull the cart when loaded. Obviously, neither of these is preferable; so let's see if we can get this set up correctly.

"Typically, the shaft mounting does not allow for any adjustment of the shafts up or down relative to the cart; however, many carts, including this one, offer two or more axle height positions that can be selected. If the shaft angle was not correct, this would require us to remove the wheels and axle in order to perform this adjustment.

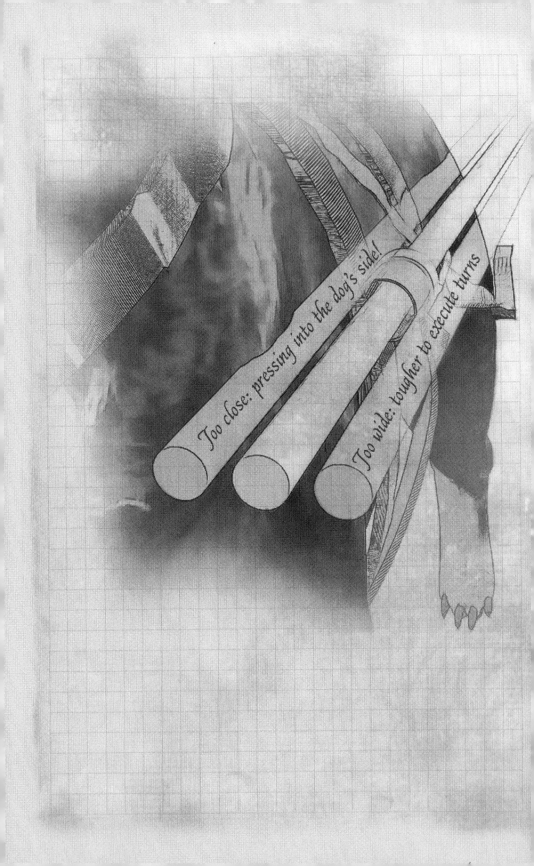

"If we needed to do this, I'd again recommend you make sure your dog is out of the harness and resting comfortably while we work.

Mike asked, "What would we do if there was not axle height adjustment?"

"Our last option would be to change the diameter of the wheels we are using. Some cart manufacturers offer two or more wheel sizes. If we needed to order replacement wheels, we'd measure the diameter of your axle and order wheels with bearings sized for your axle.

"If you happen to have a bent-shaft cart like mine, then the idea of shafts being parallel to the ground won't work for you. With the shaft located at the proper position across the point of the dog's shoulder, make sure the cart itself is parallel to the ground. If the cart was angled relative to the ground, we would use one of the adjustments we just discussed.

"Alright, now that we have the length and height set, let's take a look at the shaft width. If your cart allows you to adjust the shaft width, then set the width such that there is no more than 1-2" of clearance from each of the dog's upper arms to the inside edge of each shaft.

Mike asked, "Again, what's so special about this particular measurement?"

"This amount of clearance allows for precise turns when needed but allows the shafts not to contact the dog during normal straight pulling. If there is too much clearance at the upper arms, the dog must turn within the shafts and reach farther to be able to contact the shafts in order to turn the cart. This will result in less precise turns and often a dog that can perform a veer turn but cannot perform a pivot turn. We'll discuss these in more detail later after you get Shogun pulling.

In addition, too much clearance forces poor harness adjustment to compensate as you either must loosen the girth strap or make much longer shaft rings to reach out to the shafts. These mis-adjustments create that 'trampoline' effect we talked about earlier, and make the cart appear to bounce up and down at the dog's shoulders when it is pulled.

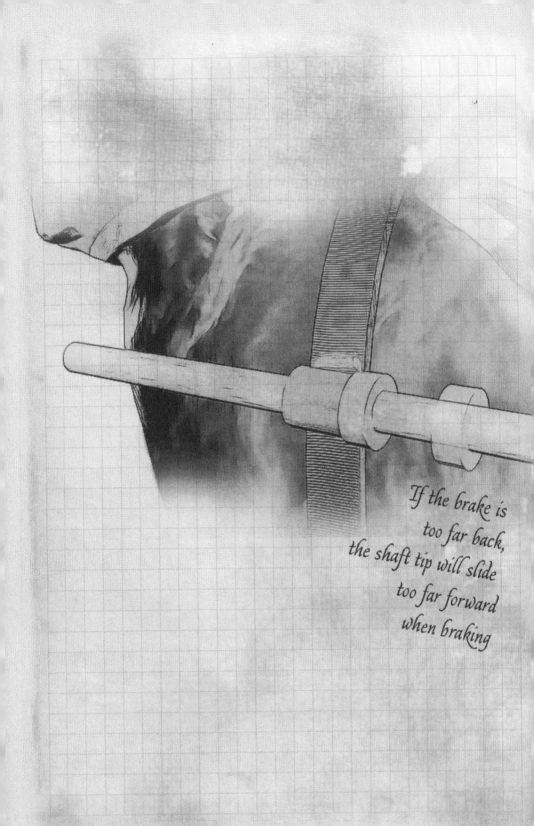

If the brake is too far back, the shaft tip will slide too far forward when braking

"Seldom is too little clearance an issue, but be aware that some dogs are not comfortable pushing their upper arms into the shafts, so constant contact could lead to reluctance to pull the cart.

"Some carts, like my bent-shaft cart, actually have grooves that allow me to slide the shafts closer or further to one another pretty easily. On your cart with the aluminum shafts, adjusting for width is just a matter of loosening the screws and rotating the shafts inward or outward as needed. Bear in mind that this type of adjustment also subtly adjusts the shaft height at the same time. As long as it's not too much, we won't have to re-perform the shaft height adjustments.

"Now, with the shaft length, height, and width set correctly, we can focus some attention on your brakes. These are devices typically positioned near the front of the shaft that prevent the shaft rings from sliding backwards beyond this point. In reality, this means that your dog itself is actually the brake since when the dog stops moving forward, the cart's momentum is stopped from moving forward as the shaft ring engages the brake on the shaft and the shaft is prevented from moving any farther forward. Brakes also allow your dog to perform backing maneuvers by forcing the shaft rings against the brakes as the dog moves to the rear.

"With Shogun standing between the shafts and the shaft rings positioned over the shafts, move the shafts forward or backwards until the desired 2-3" of shaft tip is protruding in front of the point of the dog's shoulders. Since your cart has adjustable 'shaft collars' acting as brakes, slide them forward until they contact the rear edge of the shaft rings on the harness and lock them down in position using an Allen wrench.

"Other carts like my bent-shaft cart have pre-drilled holes and some type of peg acting as the brake. My adjustment requires that I move the peg into the closest position behind the shaft rings on the harness and then I lock the pegs in place. If I needed to drill additional holes for my brake pegs, I'd mark the position immediately behind the shaft ring on the harness, drill the holes and set my brakes.

Pull the shaft rearward as you hold the girth strap

"Some carts have a fixed clip or other item that acts as the attachment to the harness. In that case, you'd position the shaft and harness and verify that there is not too much or too little protrusion of the shaft tips beyond the points of the dog's shoulders. If so, you will either need to modify the brakes or adjust the shaft length as discussed earlier.

"Now that the brakes are in place and are preventing the shaft rings from sliding backwards down the shaft, we can finally get our traces adjusted. The traces are what actually allow the dog to pull the cart forward. While there is potentially some friction of the shaft rings against the shafts, in reality the dog's harness pulls the cart forward via the traces.

"We can now attach the traces from the trace rings on the harness to the attachment point(s) on the cart or in your case, the singletree. The traces should be relatively tight. Properly adjusted traces should allow for no more than about 1 inch of movement of the shaft rings forward of the brakes when the cart is under load. To verify, I'll pull the cart slightly to the rear; watch to see how far the shaft rings move along the shafts relative to the brakes."

Mike said, "Another magic measurement. What's the purpose of this one?"

"If there is more than 1 inch of play in the traces, your starts become less precise, especially when the cart is under load. The dog starts moving forward and the shaft rings slide forward along the shaft until eventually the movement is checked by the traces when they become tight. Under heavy freight loads, this can cause a jerky motion as the dog starts forward under no load, then the load comes into play slightly later as the traces become tight. This can lead to reluctance to start pulling if the cart is under load. Properly adjusted traces allow the dog, cart and load to all begin moving forward at the same time.

"Extremely loose traces can result in a safety issue, as it is possible for the dog to move the shaft rings far enough forward along the shaft that they disengage from the shaft before the traces become tight. I recommend that handlers always verify the length of the traces under load, as the cart tends to pull backwards away from the dog, especially when moving uphill or if a wheel encounters a rut.

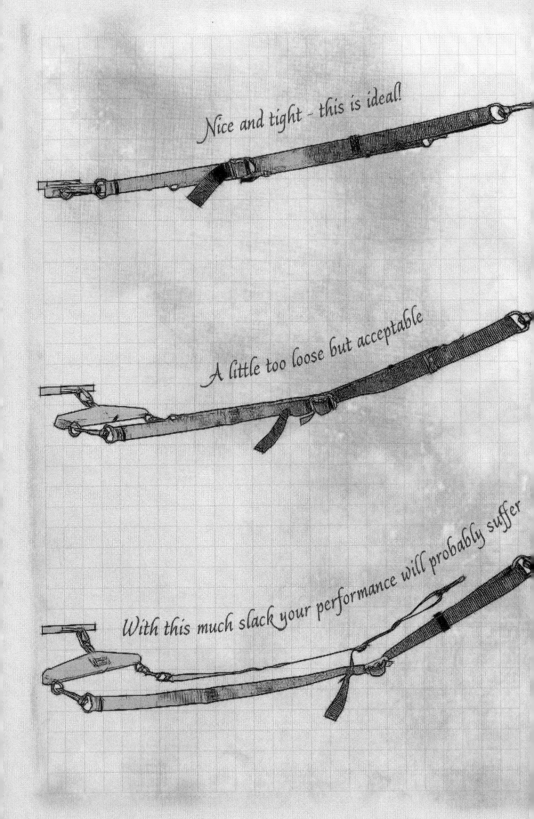

"In addition, loose traces will make your braking less precise. If the traces are loose, under load the shaft rings slide forward along the shaft and leave the immediate area of the brakes. In this case, when the dog stops, the cart continues to move forward until the shafts move forward far enough to allow the shaft rings to contact the brakes. In extreme cases, your dog has already stopped moving, and then the cart jerks itself to a halt when the brakes engage. This type of mis-adjustment can make the dog reluctant to stop the cart, especially under load.

"On your cart, your single tree is fixed into a horizontal plane by its attachment, so we can easily tighten up the traces without worrying about it. If you have a singletree that does not maintain itself on a horizontal plane, then when attached to the traces, the singletree should be "flying" or pulled tight enough to stay horizontal on its own. In addition to the other problems noted with loose traces, when combined with singletrees, the singletree can tend to flop around and make noise as it contacts the shafts, the cart, or drags along the ground.

"Many traces have a relatively complex set of buckles that allows for them to be adjusted over a large range of lengths. While this is convenient, they are often difficult to adjust when attached, so it is best to remove them from the cart and harness before proceeding. If you have to do so, it may also be a good idea to remove Shogun from the cart and let him rest while we work on the traces and get them pretty close to where we want them. It can be frustrating for many dogs to stand in position while we make multiple adjustments to the traces.

"Your dog should be able to sit and lie down while attached to the cart. Seldom does the tightness of the traces affect this ability. As you will eventually need to train for these skills at a later time, don't worry about this now, but keep it in the back of you mind that you may need further adjustments to the traces if this becomes a problem.

"With all of our preliminary adjustments in place, we will want to get a feel for how well we've done in our set-up. However, if you are working with a dog that has never pulled a cart before, resist the urge to concentrate on the adjustments, and instead focus on just getting your dog to pull the cart. We'll discuss how that should be done shortly.

"Once we get him pulling forward reliably, then we'll take a few moments to check the harness shaft ring location, the tightness of the girth strap, shaft length, shaft height, brake position, and the initial tightness of the traces. Once he is turning reliably, we'll re-check the shaft width and re-check the traces. And once he begins backing, sitting, lying down, and pulling a weight load, we'll re-check the brakes, and the traces. But we have a long way to go before we need to worry about all of that.

"Many of these final adjustments are best viewed from a distance away from your cart as the dog is working. I can work your dog for you while you watch, and you can see some of this for yourself. Alternately, getting an experienced drafter to watch you work your dog will often reveal issues and they will make suggestions. But we'll get to all of this later. For now, let's get Shogun unhitched, and unharnessed, and well rested for his next adventure. After that, it's time for him to learn how to pull."

Progression

"Did you bring the good stuff? You know we're going to need it."

"I'm not so sure about this 'good stuff'," said Mike. "Isn't a dog treat a dog treat? I mean, I've never seen him not eat one before."

"Well, you've probably never worked him through something so different and potentially stressful before, so it's good to be ready."

I had instructed Mike to bring three kinds of dog treats for our next session later in the day. First, he needed to bring a 'standard' treat, like any run-of-the-mill dog cookies or mini dog biscuits. Next, he had to up the ante — this could be one of the softer types of dog jerky, small bits of hot dog, or my old standbys, deli meat and string cheese. Finally, for the ultimate in high-value, we'd need to bring out the big guns — cooked chicken, steak, or my dog's personal favorites, bratwurst and anything smoked on the BBQ.

"So everything on the list either needs to be small, soft, or both? Shogun is usually pretty fond of that 'natural' style jerky and those hard dog biscuits."

"Yeah, we'll need to avoid anything he has to chew on. Basically, we want enough of something so they know they are getting treated, but small or soft enough that they swallow without having to pause," I said.

"So which treats do we use when?"

"Unfortunately, the answer is: 'It depends...' meaning we'll have to play that by ear. Essentially, you'll want to treat with the lowest value treat possible to still get the dog through whatever we're training them on. And don't be stingy. We're going to be asking for many new behaviors, and the treats will usually get us there. Use a steady supply of treats on his nose to make him forget he's doing something he's unsure of, and once we get something really good out of him, don't be afraid to give him a 'jackpot' of extra treats. If you have to, treat enough so that you can skip a meal later in the day."

"OK, let's review the 'progression,' as I like to call it. We talked about the fact that you can train almost any dog to draft by working through a progression of incremental steps from harnessing through hitching. Many dogs will need to work through the progression over a number of sessions that range from days to weeks. Many Berners often go directly through the progression in a single session, resulting in the dog pulling the cart almost immediately. However, there's a down side to this, which is that if or when a Berner has difficulty in the progression, it's often hard to find someone to help correct the issue, since it is typically so easy to get them pulling in most cases."

"Well, I've got a Berner, and you've already seen that he doesn't appear to be afraid of the cart in any way," said Mike, "I don't see why we don't just hitch him up and start him pulling right away."

"Yes, but it's one thing to see a cart or stand next to it, and it can be a completely different thing altogether when your dog is hitched and starting to pull. Everything in the dog's world is context based, so when they have nothing to fall back on for comparison purposes, you can get some pretty unpredictable results. For example, noises that ordinarily would never bother them if they are off-leash and running around loose can become very frightening to them once they make the connection that the noise is following them, as is the case with the cart. If they feel they can't get away, the results can be very bad. A dog that loses control and breaks from you can easily overturn their cart, which can set back your drafting by weeks or months, or potentially cause injuries.

I know you want to get going, but let's just work through each of the progression exercises for a couple of minutes, and if everything looks good, you'll have him pulling the cart in no time."

"All right, then where do we start?"

"Well, you've already completed the first steps by just getting him to wear the harness and allow you to perform adjustments on it. We discussed that this step in the progression can bother some dogs. They will attempt to chew at the harness and try to pull out of it. Had this been the case, your homework would have been to have him wear the harness around the house for brief intervals, treating as you go, until you built up time, and the harness no longer bothered him. Again, most Berners take to the harness quite willingly, and this also makes them potentially good backpackers, if you need another activity at some point in the future."

"OK, then I'll go ahead and get the harness back on him," said Mike. "What's next?"

"Believe it or not, the traces can bother a lot of dogs. Or more specifically, it's the fact that something appears to be following them, and pulling them backwards. If you think about it, for a dog that's never pulled anything in the past, traces can seem rather unnatural. But we have a few tricks up our sleeves if we need them.

"Now that you have Shogun harnessed, here's what I want you to do. Start treating him in a stand-stay. I'm going to hook the traces to the trace attachments on the harness, and I'll walk behind him as you start moving him forward. At first, I'm going to keep them rather loose and just let them rub along his flanks. Once he starts moving more consistently at a good pace following your treats, I'm going to start applying a little rearward pressure along the traces for a few seconds at a time. Hopefully, it won't bother him, and he'll just pull through the tension to get to the treats as we keep walking along.

"If he seems to get nervous with me standing so close behind him, we can do a similar exercise in another way. We'll get 10-20 feet of rope and either attach it to the trailing connectors of the traces, or remove the traces and connect the rope directly to the trace attachments on the harness. Either way, I can now stand several feet further behind, and alternately start to apply some drag as he's walking along.

One other exercise we can do here involves having him pull something from the ends of the traces. We'll need to have the item at least as wide as the dog so that the traces don't get fouled around his rear feet. I like to use a 12-18" piece of 2"-3" diameter PVC. I drilled a couple of holes at either end to allow me to attach the traces. You could also use a piece of 2" x 4" with eye bolts at either end. With you treating continuously, we'll just let the pipe follow him and drag along the ground. The curved edges make it so that it won't foul against most things we'll encounter. This is a good exercise because in addition to getting some drag from the item, it can also make some noise and because of the limited length of the traces, it needs to follow along behind him pretty closely.

"Since he only seemed mildly concerned to have someone walking behind him, he's willing to pull against the traces, and the item dragging behind him in not much of a bother, we can go to the next progression.

"So if we had any issues," Mike asked, "we'd just stop here and continue to work on these exercises until this didn't bother him, correct?"

"Absolutely. I think you're starting to see that there's a pattern to all of this. But since we're good to go, let's increase the difficulty a bit and try him with the shafts. Again, the natural inclination for the handler is to simply bring up the cart and hitch the dog to see what happens. However, there are several things we can do to ease into this a bit more slowly. Let's start by simulating the cart's shafts with lengths of PVC pipe. With a couple of sections about 4' to 6' long and 1" to 2" in diameter, we can push them up through the shaft rings and have them trailing along behind him.

Your job will be to treat and move him forward and my job will be to hold the shafts up roughly parallel to the ground. As with the traces, having a solid object rub against the dog's side and follow them around as they move is a bit unnatural, so again, your mileage will vary based upon your individual dog.

"Once he's moving OK with the shafts being carried behind him, we could rig up an attachment simulating the brakes so the shafts won't slide backwards through the shaft rings. Then we can have him start to drag the shafts around. This can be a little risky, especially if you don't do something to keep the

shafts roughly parallel to each other, such as attaching our pipe from the trace exercises. A better solution, especially if you are working without an assistant, is a set of 'pool noodles.'

"What is a 'pool noodle?' I've never heard of that," said Mike.

"Pool noodles are cylinders of foam, often around 3" in diameter and around 6' long. Kids use them as floating toys in swimming pools, but they work great for our purposes. They are extremely lightweight, and all you need to do is cut them end-on for about 6" from one end. You can then slide one side of the cut through the shaft rings, and they will pretty much clamp themselves in place. You can drag these around with less worry about weight, snagging, or noise, and if they get stuck, they will just slide out from the shaft rings on their own, so there's very little risk of injury if your dog gets spooked. Let's get these hooked up, and in this case, I'll leave you two to work through the exercise yourselves.

"So far so good. He's no more than mildly unsure of the pool noodles, but not enough to make him stop going for the treats, so I think we're ready for the next progression. Now, we've simulated about everything we can short of hitching to the actual cart, so you're finally going to get your wish. Much like working with a kid on their bike the first time you take off the training wheels, we're still going to be pretty hands-on for the time being.

"Let's get him in a stand-stay and while you're treating, I'll bring the cart up from behind him. After working with the simulated shafts, this shouldn't bother him too much at this point. Now, let's guide the shafts through the shaft rings and move the cart forward up to the brakes.

"And since we already know that the traces are adjusted pretty well," asked Mike, "we can just connect them next?"

"Well you would think so, wouldn't you? But actually, for this exercise, I'm going to recommend that we NOT attach the traces at all. There's usually some friction between the shafts and the shaft rings, so they'll do a little bit of pulling, especially since the cart is empty. And we're both going to be holding the shafts to keep as much weight off of Shogun's back as possible. But if something goes really wrong during his first cart pull, I want to have the ability to get him out of the cart as quickly and easily as possible. Without traces, we

can literally drop the cart, and he'll move forward and away from it without us having to struggle with buckles. We'll bring them along with us though, in case he progresses quickly.

"So, here's the drill – you'll stand with him in heel position, slightly behind you on your left side. Use your left hand to hold the shaft, and you can bundle up his leash and hold it there as well. With your right hand, you'll be treating, so you'll actually be moving a bit sideways as we move forward, keeping your right hand in front of his nose with those treats. I'll be on the left side, using my right hand to hold the shaft. Basically, we're going to be pulling the cart for him.

When we go, all we want to do is move forward, generally straight, for as long as he's willing to work. Initially, if we need to steer at all, you and I will do that for him by moving the shafts in the direction we need to go, and he should just follow along, as long as the treats stay in front of his nose.

"Now that he's pulling straight, as we move towards the end of the area we have to work, we can either halt him, remove him from the cart, reposition it in the direction we need to go and re-hitch, or we can 'suggest' a very large radius turn, mostly by pulling and pushing on the shafts gently in the direction we need to go. If he is willing to start making this 'veer' turn, you can start your training for turns by moving the treat to the left or right in front of his nose and allowing him to pull through to get to it. For now, let's not worry about the fact that he's turning or try to give it any command. Just keep on treating and congratulating him for pulling.

"Next, as we continue to move forward, let's slowly stop assisting on the shafts. You can drop yours first, and I'll then gradually give him more and more of the shaft weight, but I'm going to continue to stay in this position, in case something spooks him and we have to grab the cart while we settle him down. Eventually, over a few minutes of work, he should take all the weight from both shafts, and I will move slightly further away from him as we continue to work. Once it looks promising that he's not going to try to bolt and outrun the cart, we'll go ahead and get the traces on for the first time. If we've done everything correctly, he really shouldn't even notice the fact that he's just learned to pull the cart for the first time, and you've moved one step closer to that 'walk in the park' that I promised you.

"Now that we've got him pulling the cart straight on his own, and we've gotten through a couple of guided turns, let's end this on a high note. Let's get him unhitched and unharnessed, and you can give him a treat jackpot, like we discussed earlier. By the way, you'll also want to start training that he should never potty while in the harness. Depending upon any draft tests in your future, this can be problematic, and besides you have enough to worry about without dealing with a cleanup on aisle nine while the dog is hitched.

"Sometimes you have no choice, but generally speaking don't let him mark, and make sure you work in relatively short sessions where you get him unharnessed from time to time. Then try to get him to potty when he's out of the harness. After 15-30 minutes, we will hitch him up again and repeat the straight pull exercise once or twice more, and then we can call it a day."

Learn to Turn

When next we met, Mike was pretty pleased with his progress. Shogun was easily pulling the cart in straight lines, and was working through assisted turns without any difficulty.

"Too bad we can't just keep pulling straight." Mike stated. "He seems to do that really well."

"Yeah, what we've gotten so far is pretty much his instinctual behavior to pull. Everything else from here on out is going to require training, but much of it he should take to well, especially if we don't rush things and we keep those treats coming.

"Today, he's going to learn to turn. Basically there are two types of turns, and you're already working him through the first – the 'veer.' You can think of a veer as a suggestion of a direction. Basically, the dog will move slightly to the left or right, and the cart will follow along for the ride. For the most part, the harness is going to execute the turn as the dog applies more pressure to one side than the other as he heads in the direction of the treats you will be providing. Eventually, we'd like to start seeing gentle pressure being applied by his shoulder against the shaft on the side he's veering towards. You can think of the veer as your general-purpose turn since it is used to set your alignment into obstacles and for most typical maneuvering.

"The other turn is more difficult. It's called the 'pivot.' The goal of this turn is to pivot the cart around in a much smaller radius than the veer by not only

applying heavier pressure of the dog's shoulder into the shaft, but also by getting the dog to perform a 'crossover' with their feet. In a veer turn, the front feet shift left or right together, but remain parallel to one another. In a pivot turn crossover, the foot on the outside of the turn will actually reach over and cross in front of the foot on the inside of the turn. Then the inside foot will move in the direction of the turn, and the process repeats. In terms of progression, first we'll want to see strong shoulder pressure, and then we'll hope for a crossover on the front legs. Eventually, if you can get a crossover on the rear legs as well, you'll have a pivot turn that can literally spin the cart in place over the center of its axle.

"As you can guess, this is a more intermediate or advanced exercise and it's used for precise maneuvering and for getting your dog and cart through tight spots in and around obstacles. Not to mention, it looks really impressive when executed properly. But don't worry about the pivot turn too much for the time being. A good solid veer will get you far, and in fact, I'd say the majority of teams passing BMDCA draft tests do so with just a solid veer turn in their bag of tricks."

"Why wouldn't everyone want to train for both veer and pivot turns?"

"Honestly, most people probably don't think about the difference of the two. They just think about turns, and whether or not their dog can turn the cart. In other cases, it's probably not knowing how to train for a pivot turn. Bear in mind, too, that this is also a handler training exercise. Just because you might have the ability to execute a pivot turn, that doesn't mean that it's the right tool for the job every time.

For example, a pivot is excellent for getting you out of a corner, but it's not the best turn for circling an obstacle because the radius is too tight. Always remember that your team consists of you, your dog, and your cart, and all three of you need to get around an obstacle without hitting it. So, sometimes the right answer is to veer, and sometimes the right answer is to pivot. As you can imagine, this means it would be a good idea to eventually have two commands to use, one for each type of turn you want to perform.

"And here I thought we'd just be using 'left' and 'right' and Shogun would just know what to do. Sounds like it's a bit more complex."

"Well, you make an interesting point about the dog knowing what to do. Let me ask you a question. When you are just leash walking your dog, do you tell him 'left' and 'right' or do you just expect him to follow along with you based upon your body positioning? If you are not taking the opportunity to train the basic control commands including fast, slow, wait, stay, and halt while he's not hitched to the cart, what would make you think that he'd be able to do those things when he is hitched to the cart? The point is, while everything you train is context-based, make sure that your dog understands that the commands you put to behaviors work interchangeably with or without the cart.

"One other aspect to training you will probably want to consider is the use of hand signals. Drafting often occurs in noisy and distracting environments. Sometimes your dog will just not hear you, and sometimes, they forget that they are supposed to be working. Having an alternative to using just your voice is another good trick. In my case, I like to train hand signals for both left and right turns, as well as for slows, halts, and backs. It's another one of these really impressive things to watch when a handler can perform a series of exercises without talking to the dog at all. In any case, just like with voice commands, we'll want to shape the behavior we want using our treats, and once the behavior is being offered, then we can apply both a verbal command and hand signal to the behavior.

"Ok, I think I've got it. We'll start with our basic veer left and right, and when I lure him through using the treats, I'll start adding voice and hand signals. What types of commands do you like to use?"

"Well, for left and right, I use 'left' and 'right.' The more traditional commands are 'gee' and 'haw,' but very few people I've met seem to use these. As to the hand signals for turns, I don't vary much from the natural action you'll need for training the exercise in the first place. You are going to need to move Shogun's nose to the left for a left turn, and to the right for a right turn, as you are moving forward. If you think about sweeping your hand in front of his nose from the center, you've pretty much got it. I drop my hand in front of his face and sweep it in the direction I want him to go. Since you'll be doing this with treats, he should follow along. Once he's following your hand and the treat, and he's veering the cart, add your voice command for left and right.

"Let's get him harnessed and hitched and give this a try. As before, we'll both start off assisting him on his veers. You can concentrate on the treating and hand signals, and I'll gently guide the cart by the shaft until he seems to get the hang of it. If he likes the treats enough, he'll never realize he's veering until he's already done it."

After working the veers to both sides, adding in hand signals and finally voice commands, Shogun was able to navigate around the open field pretty easily. We also took this opportunity to put voice and hand commands to 'pull' and 'halt.'

"So about those pivot turns," said Mike. "When can we start working on those?"

"It's never too early in concept, and it only depends on his willingness to work. We always want to end a session on a positive note, so we'll try to get him started, but if it doesn't work out, we'll get him back on veers and end there. In order to train for a pivot, you will basically be doing the same thing as you did for a veer; however, your body position will need to be further back along his flank, and you'll really be trying to get his head to turn up over his shoulder. From a stationary position, move to one side and sweep the treat across his nose and move it up over his shoulder. His head will turn and you want to keep it just outside of his reach. In order to get the treat, he's going to need to move the cart out of the way by pushing his shoulder against the shaft.

To begin with, if he even moves the cart ½" towards you, go ahead and give him the treat. You'll want to keep working by bringing the treat farther back over his shoulder so that he needs to push the cart harder each time to get the treat. Bear in mind that many dogs don't like the feel of pushing against the shaft with their shoulder, so go slow and plan to progress gradually over a number training sessions. The more you can get him to lean into the shaft, the more likely it will be that he will figure out the front crossover on his own as he needs to essentially lunge for the treat beyond his reach. When we start out, as usual, I'll be on the off side and I'll gently assist guiding the cart around as he starts to push it in your direction.

"When I started working on pivots, I used 'hard left' and 'hard right' to distinguish the turns. I don't think I use different hand signals, but after

wide gentle veers...

eventually become...

pivots!

a while as long as I continue to have the hand signal going, my dogs will continue to turn. So for me to hand signal a pivot, I just really work the turn much more tightly based primarily on my body position relative to my dog and continue with the hand signals until the turn is fully executed.

"When you start working on turns on your own, one of the best ways to do it is if you have a section of wall or fence nearby. Get a large obstacle that is easy to move and big enough that it is easy for your dog to see. I like using a soft crate, but you can use traffic cones, or a large cardboard box if you like. Start off with the obstacle several feet away from the wall and begin executing veers between the obstacle and the wall – first to one side, and then to the other. These will look like shallow v-shaped turns. You can then continue the exercise by circling around and completing the exercise again. As you continue to work, make the v-shape more and more pronounced by heading closer to the obstacle and more directly into the wall before executing your turn.

With progress, the obstacle can be moved closer to the wall, a few inches at a time. Eventually, based upon attacking the obstacle nearly perpendicular to the wall, and the ever-smaller distance between the obstacle and the wall, your dog will have no choice but to begin executing less of a veer and more of a pivot in order to complete the turn. As usual, treat a lot, expect to hit the wall or the obstacle a few times, and end on a good note with a jackpot for the best turn of the day."

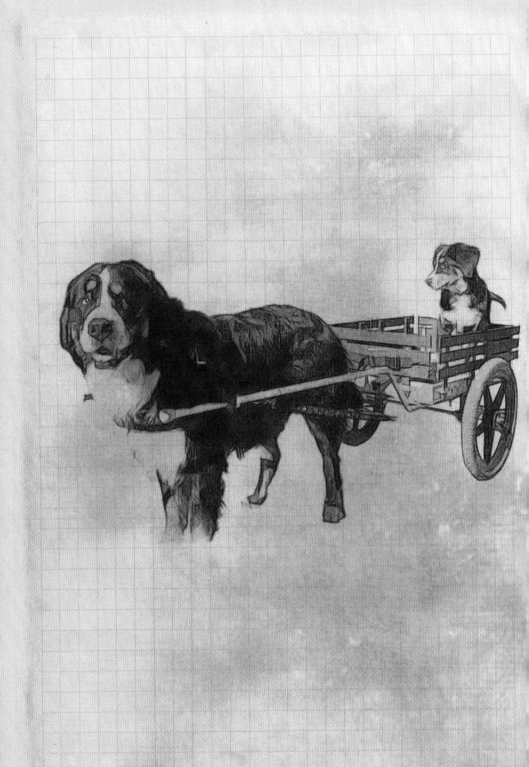

Intangibles

It had been about two weeks since we last met. "How are your practice sessions coming along?"

Mike gave me a fairly unconvincing, "Pretty well, I guess…"

"What's going on? Is he pulling and turning consistently?"

"Well, it's really the word 'consistently' that I'm having problems with. Sometimes he's working with me fine, and then the next minute, it's like I'm not even there and he's just kind of looking off into the distance."

"Ah, the 'thousand-yard stare.' I know it well. Usually this term describes unresponsive, battle-weary soldiers, but I've found it can apply to dogs as well. They just go trudging along in an unfocused manner, perfectly willing to pull, but totally unwilling to engage with their handler. It sounds like it's time to talk about the 'intangibles.'

"What exactly are the intangibles?"

"It's best to think about them as your handler's toolkit. They are things you will need to train and work on that you don't necessarily use for any particular exercise. You will need them in varying degrees, if and when something doesn't go exactly as planned. After all, there are no bad dogs, only bad handlers!"

"Well, thanks for the encouraging words. Care to elaborate on that little gem?"

Half the battle is getting your dog to pay attention to your hands!

"Actually neither portion of the phase is strictly true, but there's always some truth in most sayings. As to bad dogs, certainly there are a few who just don't enjoy the activity and probably will never progress to the degree that the handler would like. Others are not trained enough in basic obedience to succeed, but that's more of a handler issue than a dog issue. But as to bad handlers, well maybe that's better described as unprepared handlers. You're only ever going to be as good as what you know, and if you don't ever have an opportunity to practice and train with someone else, the scope of what you know may not be enough to correct many commonly occurring problems. I'm certainly not a professional dog trainer or a canine behavioral specialist, but over the years, I've learned a few tips and tricks that get me out of virtually any situation I encounter. If you don't have that big 'bag of tricks' at your disposal, you'll find yourself getting frustrated, which makes your dog frustrated, and that's so far from the 'walk in the park' idea we started with that you may find yourself wondering why you ever started drafting in the first place.

"The common theme throughout these intangibles is that you need to find the way to be the most interesting thing in the world to your dog. Since we know that it's unlikely that you can remain more interesting that everything else that your dog might encounter, you've at least got to figure out how to temporarily and immediately become more interesting than anything else. As you can guess, this is often easier said than done."

"All right, when do we begin?"

"Actually, you already have. Remember when we started training? We talked about using voice commands, or hand signals, or a combination of both, correct? Technically, I consider this a form of intangibles. If you think about it, what you are working on is giving yourself the option to do something differently when you need it. Have you been working on the hand signals?"

"Yeah, well, once Shogun started turning reliably to my voice command," Mike said, "I sort of just figured I didn't really need the hand signals anymore."

"There is some learning theory that discusses the difference between audio versus visual learning styles in humans. I don't know that I'd make the leap of faith and state that this occurs in dogs as well, but I like to think we can at least extend the concept to dogs.

"Most dogs do just fine in most circumstances with audio commands only. The problem is that 'most' is not 'all' so you are leaving yourself pretty open to the possibility of problems. Sometimes you will just encounter a very noisy environment that will make it difficult for your dog to hear you. Sometimes you know your dog could certainly hear you if they were so inclined, but there is something they are more interested in at the moment, such as a squirrel, or a leaf, of a smell.

"What I can tell you is that relying on audio commands only would be like trying to play golf with only one club in your bag. It just doesn't make sense, especially when you have the opportunity to use other techniques when appropriate. In your specific case of the thousand-yard stare, try a hand signal instead of, or in addition to the audio command, but as you've probably noticed, the audio command is being ignored anyway."

"You taught me hand signals for left and right. Is there something else I should be using for this," asked Mike.

"The thousand yard stare concept usually has them pulling steadily forward despite you asking for a turn, so if you need to turn, then use the hand signals for left and right as I've already shown you. The key to this, in my mind, is the fact that the hand signals must interrupt their vision. This means you have to get the hand signals up in front of their face for them to be effective. If the dog can't see them, and they're already unwilling or unable to hear you, you won't accomplish anything.

"Yeah, I get it. Three feet behind and two feet above Shogun's head, just isn't going to get me anywhere."

"So true. Now, if the thousand-yard stare is resulting in your dog just randomly stopping while pulling and looking off into the distance, I would try a different hand command. Basically for this one, I just start over the top center of the head and sweep my hand directly downward. Again, this breaks their vision on whatever they are looking at, and typically they will then turn and look to you for their next command. Alternatively, hand signals for left or right can still work in this circumstance if you have a little room to maneuver, as often a small change of direction can be all it takes to get your dog working again.

"On freight hauls, my dog, Watson, will often just want to lock in on a trail or road and he'll start picking up the pace to race ahead since he thinks he knows where we're going. In these cases, I will sometimes put him into a slalom where I alternate left and right hand signals to get him weaving from side to side. This often gets him refocused and working for me again."

"Got it. What's next?"

"Next? Well, I would say your posture. That's not to say that there's anything wrong with it, it's just that you essentially want more than one. Basically, it doesn't matter what your standard posture is when working with your dog. Some people will naturally be more upright, and some will tend to crouch down to be closer to the dog's head. Whatever works for you in most circumstances is fine. The key here it to find something distinctly different for when you really need to get their attention back on you. If you are naturally pretty upright, then crouching down and 'getting into your dog's face' can be a pretty effective tool. Similarly, if you already tend to work low where they can see you, then suddenly standing up to full height can have the effect of having the dog look back over their shoulder to see what you are up to.

"Along with posture, you will also want to consider your volume and tone of voice. Again, just examine what usually works for you and then work to find something different for when you need it. If you are usually loud, then try to get low and whisper to your dog. If you are normally quiet, then suddenly getting loud may have the desired effect. This is not meant to imply that you should be yelling at and berating your dog, but you can certainly have a tone and volume reserved for situations where you want no nonsense from your dog.

"The opposite of having a good range of tone and volume options is the 'monotone handler.' No matter what is happening or what they need from their dog at any given moment, this handler uses exactly the same tone and volume, often to no avail. And this isn't meant to imply that these guys always sound like the cartoon character Droopy Dog. I've seen handlers who were so constantly upbeat and up-tempo that their dogs had no way of knowing they had just done something incorrectly. In either case, much like the continuous buzzing of an annoying fly, after a while, your dog essentially can no longer hear you because everything sounds exactly the same in all circumstances.

"As I've mentioned, the main point is to do whatever you need to do to get your dog's attention back on you, and there's all kinds of options you can mix in as well. These include clapping your hands, tapping you hand against the outside of your thigh, whistling, or making any other kind of funny noise you can think of. Don't rule out having a running conversation with your dog – anytime their attention is wavering, start chatting again, but mix it up and avoid that monotone. I even heard of a guy who sang to his dog the during entire freight haul."

"Well, that's a lot to take in," said Mike. "How do I know what to use and in what circumstances?"

"That's what practice is for. You never know what's going to get your dog's attention back until you try it, and what works one day or in one situation is likely to change over time. Don't be afraid to experiment, and keep the tricks that work. However, you don't want your attention-getters to be truly random. You kind of want to sort them in your head and save certain ones for certain situations.

"I like to think of this list as 'ask,' 'tell,' and 'demand.' 'Ask' is used for your routine 'walk in the park' circumstances. I'll ask for a left or right turn, or for a halt, and if it takes a step or two to get done, it's no big deal. If you are losing attention in these types of situations, you want to use your biggest assortment of low-value attention-getters.

"For 'tell,' these are situations where the precision or timing of the exercise is more important. I'll typically 'tell' my dog that they need to do a pivot turn, or a precise halt. For these you will want a smaller selection of your higher-value attention-getters. I don't want to imply that the only time you would use these 'tell' attention-getters is in a competition. Again, remember the monotone issue, so if everything you want your dog to do is equally important, you've just described 'normal' and 'tell' really loses its effect over time.

"Finally, there is 'demand.' You might think of these as almost life-and-death moments, such as when your dog is near a busy road, and you absolutely positively do not want them getting any closer to traffic. In competition, I save this for freight hauls with heavy weight loads. Sometimes you reach an uphill and your dog is convinced that there is no way they can pull the cart any

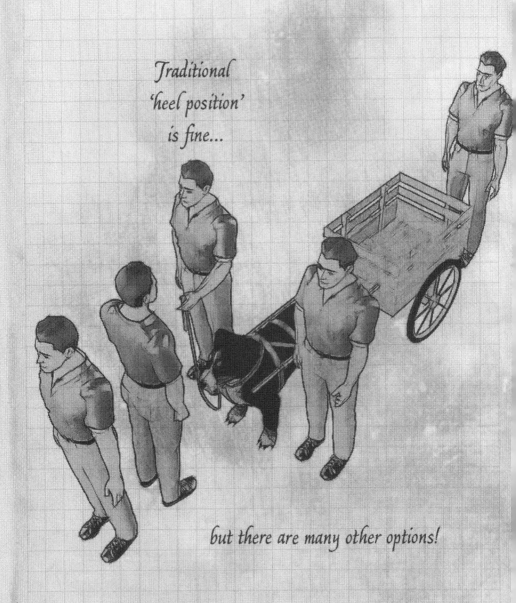

longer. In these cases, I have only one or two 'demand' attention-getters that I use only for these specific situations. Surprisingly, the one for the freight hauls is actually pretty quiet and un-dramatic. I put my dogs into a down stay and I kneel in close and quietly tell them that they only get a couple of seconds of rest and that they know they have to work again and that there is no way they aren't going to be able to pull the cart up the hill. Ten seconds later, they get a pretty loud, 'OK, pull it!' And they do.

"Wow, that's pretty cool," said Mike. "How did you ever figure that out?"

"Do you remember that movie, City Slickers, with Billy Crystal and Jack Palance? There is a scene where Curly the cowboy, asks Mitch the city-slicker, 'Do you know what the secret of life is?' He holds up one finger. 'One thing. Just one thing.' Mitch asks, 'But, what is the one thing?' Curly says, 'That's what you have to find out.' Every dog has their 'one thing,' but they don't come with user manuals, so you just have to experiment until you find what works. It can be your tone, posture, command, attitude, a combination of all of the above, or who knows what else. You just have to keep working with them until you find it."

"Is there anything else I should add to my bag of tricks while I'm at it?"

"There's always something else to try. One thing that many people forget, especially those used to conformation or obedience work, it that there is typically no requirement in drafting that the dog remain in perfect heel position on your left side. In fact, the BMDCA rules state that, 'you can work beside, behind, or in front of the dog, or any combination of these.' I would recommend trying this out sooner rather than later, and get Shogun used to you being on all sides. In addition to this being helpful in a practical drafting sense since you sometimes just can't alter your approach to certain obstacles, it is also helpful for a variety of the actual competition exercises, which we'll discuss in more detail later. If you don't bring this into you practices early, then often you have difficulty re-training as no matter where you attempt to position yourself, the dog will attempt to get back into proper heel position.

"Another trick pertains to repetition of commands. Sometimes, for reasons no handlers understand, your dog will spontaneously forget how to do something basic and simple that you've done a thousand times, such as 'sit,' or 'back.'

They just stare at you with completely blank expressions, and it can feel like you're suddenly speaking a foreign language. In these cases, despite the 'ask,' 'tell' and 'demand' escalation I taught you, you may find yourself in a situation where the command you want to give is meaningless to your dog at that moment. My suggestion is to use no more than three of the same command in a row. If you are just not getting any response and they are not even trying to execute what you want, then try something else. For example, if your dog won't sit from a stand, tell them to down instead. And if your dog won't back, try asking them to sit or down. If you can get your dog to execute a different action to a different command, they will often start working for you again, and perhaps the command that they forgot will suddenly be remembered.

"The final thing I want you to start thinking about is weaning Shogun off the treats. Eventually you want them drafting because they enjoy doing it, and not because you are continually bribing them to perform. I know we've made a big deal about treating early and often, but once you've really shaped the behaviors you want and have them reliably under voice or hand control, you'll want to start cutting off treats for 'expected' behaviors. Remember, if you ever decide to get into competitions, you can't have any treats with you inside the ring or on the freight haul. In a more practical sense, even during a 'walk in the park,' you don't want to end up at the opposite end of the park with your dog on strike because you've run out of treats or accidentally left them at home.

"At this point, 'pull,' 'halt,' 'left,' and 'right' are routine, so let's start cutting down and eventually stop treating for these. Instead, you'll save your treats for continuing to tighten up those pivot turns with 'hard left,' and 'hard right,' and for any new exercises we start working on. What I would recommend is focusing on the big jackpot treat after you've completed your workout. This you can continue to do as a replacement for all of the individual treats throughout the exercises as they are performed. That way, your dog knows that once they've finished a drafting session, they are going to get rewarded, and this will work out better for you in the end.

"I think that's enough for now, let's get the dogs harnessed and hitched, and we'll start putting some of these intangibles to good use. Hopefully, we'll be able to break that thousand-yard stare habit pretty quickly."

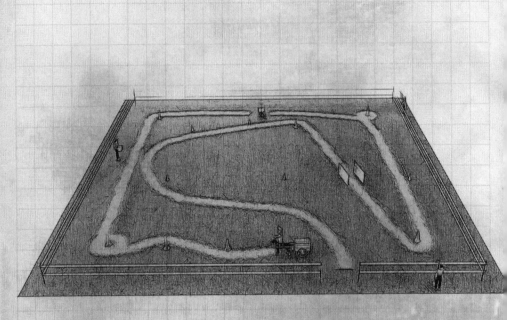

A basic draft ring

I knew from my very first moment of watching a draft test that this was going to be 'my' dog event. My wife was already learning how to show for Confirmation, and we hadn't even begun to think about Obedience, Rally Obedience, or Agility yet, although now she does all of these too. There was something in the fact that these dogs were doing exactly what they were originally bred for that made drafting very alluring to me, and of course trying to imagine how anyone could possibly ever train their dogs to perform all of these wonderful tricks with a cart was beyond my ability to comprehend. My first dog and Berner, Gandalf, was a really big, strong boy, but when I look back to a never-ending series of puppy obedience classes, I now wonder who was really training whom. Let's just say he was a bit of a handful, and we'll leave it at that.

So we started learning about drafting at one of our club's "Working Dog Day" events, and with some instructions and a borrowed cart from our breeder, I started training to the best of my ability, which it turns out wasn't very much. I chickened out on being the first to show him at one of our local draft tests and asked our breeder, who is an experienced handler and draft judge to show him instead. After all, how bad could it be? On the BMDCA Draft Test judge's Worksheet, there are ten sections that are all scored Pass/Fail. You have to pass all of the sections to get an overall passing performance. Gandalf managed to fail in six separate sections, which might possibly be some kind of record, for an untold number of individual issues. I saw this as a minor set-back, leaving room for improvement.

I worked with him for the next six months and showed him myself at the next local test, failing only four sections of the Worksheet. Six months later, we failed only two sections of the worksheet, and six months after that, we failed only one section of the worksheet. At our next test six months later and two years after we started, we finally passed, earning our first Novice Draft Dog title.

This would be an obvious allegory for the concept of, 'If at first you don't succeed, try, try again,' the value of persistence, and a never-say-die attitude. However, the reason I tell this story is something altogether different. When you fail a draft test, you have the opportunity to train and work with your best friend to correct specific issues as they arise. For some dogs, they can't or won't

execute a specific exercise repeatedly, or on a specific day. For others, it seems there is always something random where once you correct something, they stop performing something else that was already working fine. Dealing with these issues got me down from six failures to four, to two, and then to one. Just on the law of averages alone, I should have passed the next test, but I believe it was something else entirely.

What was the difference between failing and passing? Baseball legend and Hall of Fame member, Yogi Berra, is generally attributed as having said, "Baseball is ninety percent mental and the other half is physical." I had been going through the motions of drafting, but I never really thought I would pass the test because there was always going to be something new that Gandalf was going to do to trip us up. Call it lack of confidence. Perhaps I didn't have my game face on. Or you could say that I had mastered the fifty percent of the event that was the physical part of going through the motions, without having mastered the ninety percent that was the mental part of the test.

I believe I passed the first test I entered where I KNEW that I would pass before I ever set foot in the ring. Over the two years it took me to really learn to draft, I built up my toolkit from empty to full with the various tips and tricks and techniques I am explaining to you in this book. I got to the point where I KNEW there was nothing that Gandalf could do during the draft test that I didn't already know how to deal with.

I've passed a pretty good number of draft tests at this point, but that doesn't mean that I don't still occasionally fail one here or there. It is, after all, still a very difficult thing to be 'perfect' when any given dog on any given day can still surprise you, and most of the time it turns out to be the handler's fault anyway. But when you take that ninety percent mental portion out of the equation, what you have left is 'just a walk in the park.' As long as you remember that you are there doing the most fun thing you can ever do with your dog, how bad can it really be?

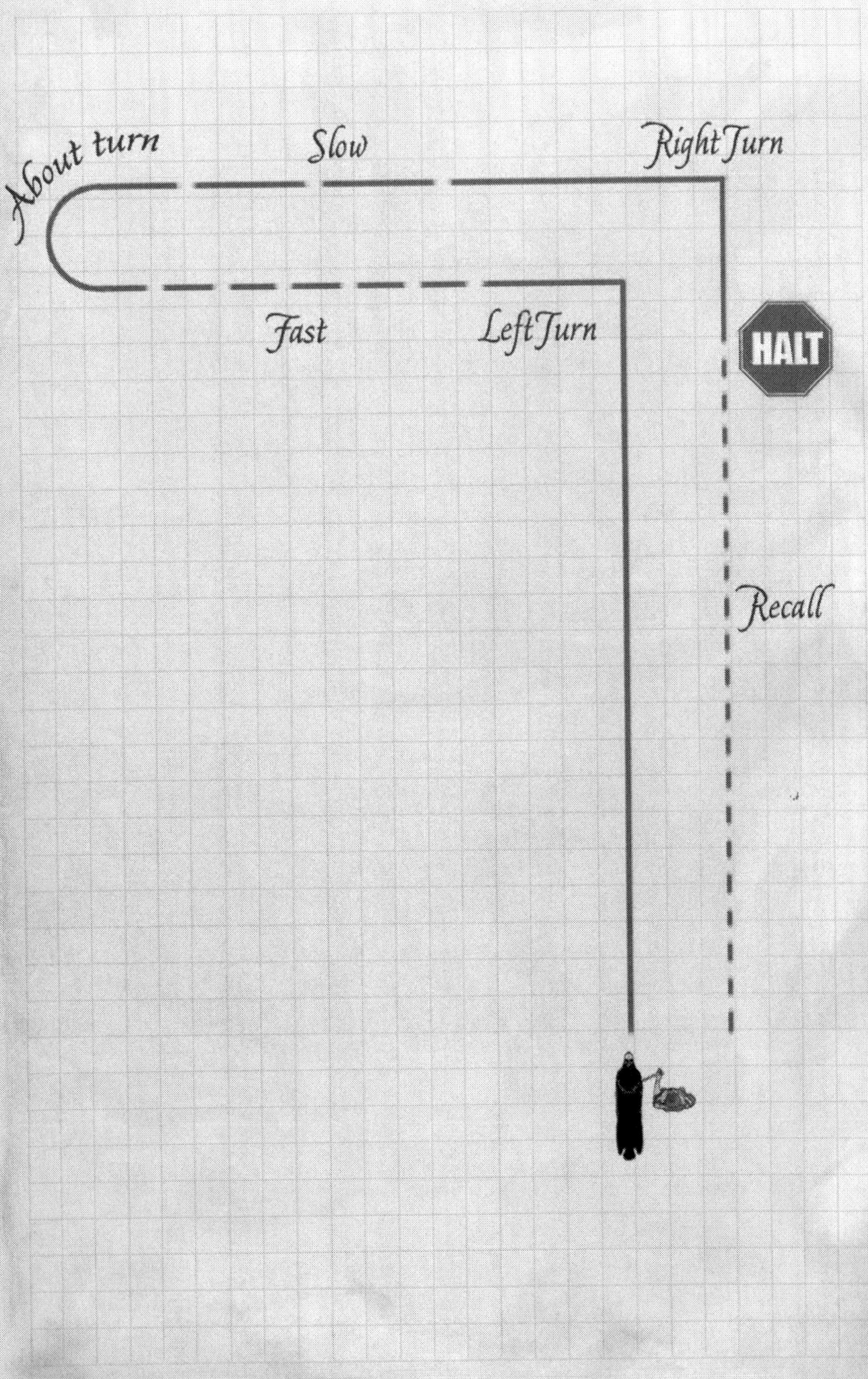
About turn
Slow
Right Turn
Fast
Left Turn
HALT
Recall

Basic Control

We met at the park again two weeks later. Mike had been working with Shogun during the evenings as well, and he said he was pretty happy with his progress on the intangibles, and now had a small, but ever growing assortment of tricks that seemed to work for getting Shogun's attention back when he needed it. Slowly but surely, the thousand-yard stare was becoming a thing of the past.

"Before we start adding additional drafting exercises to your practice sessions, the next things I want you to start working on are the 'Basic Control' exercises. These are essentially a small assortment of simple obedience exercises that are performed before you ever harness and hitch your dog. For the Berner and Newfie tests, these are included as pass/fail exercises at the beginning of the test.

"In prior versions of the BMDCA Draft Regulations, all of the classes had to start their tests with the Basic Control exercises. In the 2011 rules, this was changed so that only the Novice class has to perform the Basic Control exercises. The logic behind this is that you must pass a test in the Novice Class before progressing to any of the other classes. Having passed Novice, you have demonstrated the ability to perform Basic Control, and therefore it is not required for the other classes.

"Personally, whether you ever choose to compete or not, I would advise that you start all of your future draft practice sessions with the Basic Control exercises. Just like putting the drafting collar on your dog, and putting the harness on your dog, adding Basic Control to your preparation for getting your dog to work will give you one more set of steps in your ritual of preparation.

If you always start your sessions the same way, and you reinforce them with commands like, 'Let's get ready to work,' or 'It's time for drafting,' then your dog should be one hundred percent ready to work for you once you complete the hitching."

"OK,' said Mike, 'you mentioned that these are simple obedience exercises. I know a few people who have earned Companion Dog titles, and I know that competition obedience can be pretty unforgiving. Is this the same as that?"

"Luckily, the Basic Control exercises are based upon the heeling patterns and recalls from obedience competition, but they tend to be judged a bit less rigorously, and you can use multiple voice and/or hand signals throughout most of the Basic Control exercises, as opposed to having your dog key in to only your body language.

"The first set of exercises are considered Walking Under Control and consist of the commands 'Forward,' 'Slow,' 'Fast,' 'Normal,' 'Right turn,' 'Left turn,' 'About turn,' and 'Halt.' Technically these can be performed in any order or pattern subject to the space available within the draft ring, but these are usually performed as a heeling-style 'L' pattern with the slow or fast on the outbound portion of the bottom of the 'L' and the opposite on the return after the about turn. You are usually asked to 'Halt' just after you complete the return on the bottom of the 'L' so that you end facing where you started and at least 40 feet away. The second exercise consists of a Recall, where you leave your dog and then call them to you, usually back to where you started the Basic Control exercises, which in the BMDCA test is also typically the location of the Harness and Hitch exercise.

"Before we dive into all of this a little deeper, here are a couple of items to compare and contrast from the various tests. For the BMDCA test, you will perform these Basic Control exercises in the draft ring as part of your individual performance just prior to proceeding with the maneuvering exercises that include your draft rig. Up to six dogs will complete their individual performances in order, before proceeding to the Group Stay and Freight Haul. Since Basic Control is only performed in the Novice Class, you will perform these exercises on leash, with the exception of the Recall, of course.

"For the Newfie test, which is fairly similar to the Berner test, they set up a separate smaller ring specifically for the Basic Control exercises. You will perform individually for the Basic Control and Recall, but they add a group One Minute Down Stay at the end of the individual exercises, and a group of up to ten dogs will return to the ring to complete this exercise. Dogs will then harness and hitch and perform individually in the maneuvering ring before performing their group stay and freight haul in groups of no more than six dogs. Since the Newfies have only a single class level, which combines some apsects of the Berner Novice and Open classes, you will enter the ring on leash, but perform the exercises off leash. They've also recently dropped the requirement for 'Slow' and 'Fast' from their Basic Control.

"The Rottie test is quite a bit different, and they do not have any specific Basic Control exercises. They begin with individual Harness and Hitching, then individual performance of the maneuvering course, and finally a Group Down Stay with no more than eight dogs."

"So just like anything else we've been working through, I assume there are tips and tricks for the Basic Control exercises?" asked Mike.

"For the BMDCA test, the biggest item to work on for the Novice class is leash control, and this is certainly a concern for the Basic Control exercises, especially since this forms the judge's first opinion of the working capability of your team."

"Well, in the past,' said Mike, "I would have assumed that 'leash control' meant not dropping your leash when your dog runs away from you, but I suppose that you have a different definition in mind."

"Yes, specifically, I'm talking about the differences between 'J' leash, tight leash, and leash guidance. 'J' leash is what the judges are looking for in your performance, and it describes the way that the leash hangs down from your hands, and then curls back up to the dog's collar, in the shape of the letter 'J.' Essentially this shape is indicative that there is always sufficient slack so that you can ensure that your dog is responding to your voice or hand commands and is not being pulled through the exercises by the leash. When you pull the leash hard enough to yank your dog's collar and essentially force them to do something that they otherwise would not have done, this is called 'leash

The Near-Hand Leash

The Far-Hand Leash

guidance.' Somewhere in the middle is 'tight leash,' when all of the slack has come out of the 'J' and the leash now forms a straight line between the handler and the dog.

"As an example, imagine a handler with a nice 'J' leash walking in a straight line with their dog. Imagine the handler calling for a right turn and moving away from their dog to the right. The dog doesn't execute the command and continues to move ahead in a straight line. The 'J' leash disappears and reaches the point of tight leash. If the handler realizes the situation, they should return to their dog, re-establish the 'J' leash, and then re-issue the command to turn. If the handler doesn't realize the situation, the tight leash can easily become leash guidance, as the next thing that happens is that the dog is yanked to the right to start the execution of the turn.

"You will be failed in your test for leash guidance and these instances are usually pretty easy for the judge to detect. Judges prefer black and white situations. A 'J' leash that's easy to see - great you're passing. Leash guidance – that's unfortunate and you're now failing, but this too is a pretty easy call to make. Tight leash – well, judges really hate to deal with this situation, especially as it tends to be repetitive throughout a performance. Every time a judge sees the slack go out of the 'J' and the leash becomes tight, you force a judgment call as to whether the tight leash constituted leash guidance. You might pass with several comments on the judge's worksheet to 'Watch the tight leash!' or you might fail for having one or more instances of leash guidance. The point is, it's best to not make the judges have to think about what they just did or did not see relative to your leash work.

"All right then, how do we improve our leash work?"

"Here are a couple of things to keep in mind. Most people who work with their dog in traditional heel position will keep the leash in the hand closest to the dog. Since we've already discussed being able to work both sides of your dog, you'll want to get comfortable handling the leash in either hand. In addition, since I've got you using hand signals, my suggestion is to work with the leash in the hand furthest away from the dog. This keeps the hand closest to the dog available for both hand signals and for practice treats when needed and keeps you in a decent posture relative to the dog.

"If you work with the leash in the hand closest to the dog and try to use hand signals with your outside hand, you'll find yourself forever trying to get slightly in front of your dog so you can turn towards them and bring your outside hand around in front of their face. This just looks awkward and it's never a good idea to turn your back on where you're trying to go.

"Once you've settled on which hand to use and when, you'll want to work on being able to reel in and pay out leash quickly and effortlessly. Start in heel position; set your 'J' shape, and reel up the extra into your hand. Ideally, the distance between you and your dog should remain constant throughout, so the size and shape of the 'J' would also remain constant and it is described as being within arm's length at all times. However, you will often find the distance changing slightly, depending upon terrain, obstacles and the responsiveness of your dog. Many beginning handlers just seem to lock in on their initial leash length and hold it in a death-grip throughout. Failure of the handler to adjust to the dog's position and to change the relative length of leash will result in tight leash and leash guidance situations.

"One of the ways you are going to exhibit teamwork is that you will continually adjust and readjust your position relative to your dog to keep that arm's length distance and resetting back to that ideal 'J' leash shape. If you find your dog drifting away from you, you can avoid a tight leash by paying out some of the extra leash in your hand while at the same time, you will be repositioning yourself to start closing the gap. As the gap narrows, you will begin reeling back in the extra and the result will be that you've returned the leash shape to exactly what you started with. Temporarily the size of the 'J' got wider, but this is acceptable if you are still within arm's length of your dog, and far preferable to a tight leash.

"Two situations highlight problems with leash control and ultimately, teamwork. The one I described in my example of leash guidance, I often call the 'pivot point.' In that example, the handler issued the command for a turn and expected that the dog would execute the turn. If the handler remains at the location the command was issued as the pivot point to the turn, but never adjusts their position or the length of their leash when the dog does not respond, the leash will go tight and the turn will be executed only due to leash guidance.

"A similar situation is when the handler calls for a halt and 'stops on a dime' at the location they expected their dog to stop as well. As before, if the dog doesn't respond to the command and the handler's location and leash length don't change to correct the issue, the result will be a halt with tight leash or leash guidance.

"Now, as to the Basic Control exercises themselves, hopefully you've been training these since the time you started your puppy obedience classes. At the start of the sequence, you will come into the ring, and will move to the location the judge points out so that you can start the exercises. Establish your initial location and have your dog settle into position. Most handlers will sit their dog in heel position, usually as one of those ritual items we discussed to signal to the dog that now is the time to work; however, there is no specific provision that the dog start in any particular position, so you could begin in a stand-stay or down-stay if you feel that is more stable for your particular dog. The judge will then ask, 'Are you ready?' This is not meant to be a trick question, but many handlers feel that there is an obligation to immediately agree and proceed. If you are not ready, tell the judge, and take a moment or two to reposition or circle and re-settle your dog. As long as the dog is generally in control and responding to your commands, the judges will typically not hold this against you.

"Once you are ready, notify the judge; this can be verbally or with the nod of your head. The judge will then give the command 'Forward.' At this point, you can issue whatever command you want in order to get your dog moving forward. As with most of the judge's commands throughout the test, it is the concept being judged, not your use of a corresponding command. So instead of 'Forward,' you can use whatever you want, including, 'Let's go,' or 'Time to work,' or you can just start moving forward if your dog will follow your body language alone.

"From that point onward, you will need to listen and respond to the judge's commands. Prior to the start of the actual test, the handlers are provided the opportunity for a walkthrough of the maneuvering and freight haul courses, and this includes the location and order of exercises for Basic Control. If you pay attention, you will know roughly when and where each of the other commands will be given. Don't anticipate the commands – just respond as you

hear them. In some order, depending upon the available room for the exercise and the layout of the course, you will get the remaining commands. For the 'Right turn,' and 'Left turn,' these should be executed as 90-degree turns. Military precision is not required, but long sweeping curves are not the same thing as executing the turn at the command.

"For the 'Fast,' 'Slow,' and 'Normal,' you will usually get one of the speed changes on the way out on the 'L' pattern, followed by a return to 'Normal.' Whichever speed change you didn't get going out, will be asked for on the way back, again followed by a return to 'Normal.' In order to perform the exercises correctly, you need to show distinct changes of pace going into and out of the speed change commands. This does not mean that the handler slows while the dog proceeds as before – you both need to execute and demonstrate the changes in pace, again using whatever commands work for you and your dog. If your dog happens to normally be either a very fast or very slow worker, it may be necessary to think about what speed you need to maintain as 'Normal.' Again, you are not being judged here on the definitions of 'Fast,' and 'Slow,' but on the changes of pace associated with moving from one speed to the next.

"Somewhere in the pattern, usually at the far end of the 'L,' you will be asked to demonstrate an 'About turn.' This usually implies what is called a 'Right about turn,' in which case you act as the pivot point for the turn and your dog moves around you as you rotate to your right. The rules don't specify that you can't do a 'Left about turn,' in which case the dog is the pivot point as you move around in a half-circle to your left, but it would be pretty uncommon to see this. Eventually, you will execute whichever 90-degree turn you hadn't previously done, and you will be asked to 'Halt,' and then the judge will end the exercise with 'Exercise finished.' This completes the first portion of Basic Control with most common issues being no discernable changes of pace and tight least/leash guidance.

"For the Recall exercise, you will usually start at or near the location of your 'Halt,' depending upon whether there is enough distance remaining to allow the approximately 40 feet of recall required. If the judge asks you to reposition, just follow their instructions. It used to be required that the dog start the Recall exercise in sitting position, but in the 2011 Edition of the Draft Test Regulations, that was changed to allow the dog to start in any position. Some

handlers do not read their rule books, and often think that the exercise must start in a sit, which can cause confusion and frustration if your dog has decided that on that particular day, they no longer understand the command 'Sit.' In any case, you will be asked to remove your leash and hand it to either a judge or steward. This usually happens while you re-settle and position your dog, and prior to the command, 'Are you ready?' As before, it is up to you to decide if you are truly ready and until you are and until the judge issues their next command, 'Leave your dog,' you may continue to talk to you dog and give them whatever commands are necessary to get them prepared for the Recall.

"Once the 'Leave your dog' command is given by the judge, you may only issue a single command and/or signal in order to get your dog to wait. This means you can do a voice command, a hand signal, or a combination of the two, but they must be issued simultaneously. The concept of 'Wait' is what is being judged, not the command you use. A 'Wait' means that the dog can change their position, but cannot change their location. This means that your dog can sit from a stand, or down from a sit, or rise up from a down, as long as they do not move from their original location. So as you start to walk away, if you see them change position, don't react to it, and don't return to your dog and issue another 'Wait.' If you do, you have issued a double command, and you will fail the exercise.

"As you can imagine, the change of position ends up being a judgment call as to whether the location changed while the position changed, so the recommendation is to practice a lot to ensure your dog reliably holds their position. The reason I mention this, is that after you leave your dog, and walk the longest 40 feet of your life, when you spin around to face your dog, and realize that they are not in the position you left them in, many handlers assume that they have failed the exercise, and give up on the rest of the test. Never assume that you know what the judge saw and always proceed with the rest of your exercises as if you are passing. If you've already failed, there is nothing you can do about that, but you can certainly get in a good practice run for the remainder of your time in the ring."

"Have you ever seen that at a test, where a handler assumes they've failed?" asked Mike.

One... and Only One... Recall Command

"Unfortunately, it happens far more often than you would think and the handler is often disappointed with their effort later once they realized they were passing until the point they made another mistake. OK, so you've issued your single command for your 'Wait,' you've left your dog at the judge's command, and you've moved to the Recall location where you're now facing your dog. The judge will issue the 'Call your dog' command, which can be verbal, or a hand signal, or a combination of both. The judge standing closest to your dog will often not want to use a verbal command at this point as it may startle your dog during their 'Wait,' so during the walkthrough, ensure you understand how your judges will be calling the exercise that day.

"Once you have been given the command, you may now issue a single command and/or signal in order to get your dog to recall to you. As soon as your dog responds to the command and is now heading for you, you may issue as many other commands as needed to get the dog to end the exercise within arm's reach of the handler. Make sure you do not move your feet; however, as this can be interpreted that you needed to go to the dog, rather than the dog recalling to you. The judge will end the exercise with 'Exercise finished.' Sits and finishes are not required. At this point, the judge will return your leash, or you may gently guide your dog by the collar to begin the Harness and Hitch exercises.

"Sometimes your dog will not respond to the single command/signal combination and this starts the longest waiting game of your life. Strictly speaking, this is an untimed exercise, but the reality is that eventually the judges will need to proceed with the rest of the test. Ironically, if your dog is extremely obedient and they just didn't hear the command, you will likely fail, as they will remain in their 'Wait' forever. If your dog is a little less obedient, or heard the command and just decided not to execute it until they felt like it, then eventually they may start moving on their own, and as soon as they do, you can issue additional commands and complete the exercise.

"For these reasons, I have a couple of recommendations. First, always take the opportunity to issue both a voice and signal command of some sort. Since there is often a lot of noise and distractions, expect that at this distance your dog might not hear you.

And now as many commands as it takes!!

"For this, my hand signal for the Recall is a big long sweeping rise from down by my side to up and across my chest. I combine this with an exaggeratedly loud Recall command, in my case, my dog's name immediately followed with 'Here!'

"Finally, take the opportunity to control the exercise. Just because the judge has issued the command, 'Call your dog,' doesn't mean you are obligated to start the exercise immediately. I always want to make sure I have good eye contact with my dog before I start my recall sequence. If you look over and your dog is looking off in another direction, don't issue your commands, instead wait a few seconds, and usually whatever they were fixated on has gone. Once they return their attention to you, issue your commands. Alternatively, if you think they may not return their attention to you, because that squirrel is far more interesting, you can try your commands to see if you can break them out of their lack of attention, but this is certainly risky and not ideal.

"Again, at some point, the judges need to continue with the rest of the test, so you only have a relatively short window in which to comply with their command, but you may as well try for your best opportunity to succeed by having your dog's attention on you when you start. Failures during the Recall most often happen with double commands on the 'Wait' or 'Recall,' the dog changing location before the 'Recall,' or the dog not returning to the handler which often includes them running out of the ring."

"And all of this," asked Mike, "is going to make me a better drafter?"

"Well, if nothing else, it will improve your teamwork and will give you that warm-up ritual which should get your dog into the right frame of mind to be ready to draft. After that, it's up to you and Shogun."

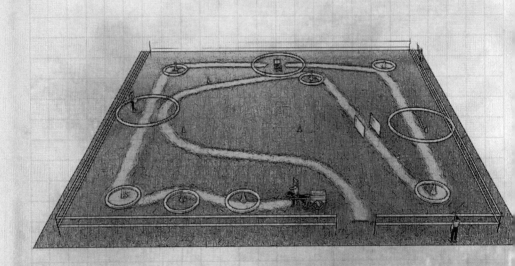

*A basic draft ring
with turns, halts and waits highlighted*

Building on Turns, Halts, and Waits

Later that day, after several practice runs through Basic Control and Recall, Mike and Shogun were ready for some drafting.

"Let's start with the harness and hitch, but this time we'll do it the same way as we'd do it as a BMDCA draft test exercise. This is the first thing you need to do to get your dog ready to draft, so it is a pass/fail exercise that determines your capability to get your harness onto the dog and get the dog hitched to the cart, effectively and safely, while keeping your dog calm and willing to work for you."

"Is this really any different than what we've already been doing each time we've harnessed and hitched for the past few weeks?" asked Mike.

"The harness and hitch process itself is pretty much identical. There are a few conventions you will need to adhere to as you work through it. First, when you enter in the Novice class, your dog will be on leash and you will commence your ring performance with the Basic Control and Recall exercises as we've already discussed. A steward, prior to you entering the ring, will place your draft cart in the ring, pointing in the direction that the judge's direct. For the most part, you will perform your Recall heading back to a location near the shafts of your cart. At this time, your dog will be off leash, and you will be anywhere from a few feet to a few yards away from your cart. You will need to get your harness out of your cart, but he first thing you will need to do is figure out what you want to do with your dog."

"What do you mean?" asked Mike.

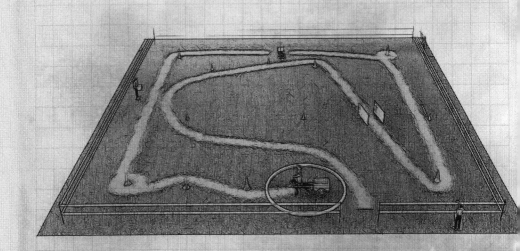

Harness and Hitch area

"Well, you now have your dog within arm's reach, and the judge will usually return your leash to the cart, so you need a plan for where you want to work while harnessing, and how you are going to get your harness out of the cart before you do so. The rules allow gentle guidance by the collar at this time, so figure out if you plan to move your dog to the cart, or your cart to the dog. You can bring your dog directly to the side of the cart and grab the harness out of the cart, or you may place your dog in a 'Stay' while you leave them to get the harness. If you elect to use a 'Stay,' pick a position that your dog will hold without moving. For this reason, many people will choose to use a 'Down Stay.'

"You will know the direction you will be heading for the first exercise following the harness and hitch, so one option is to point the dog in that direction which will make it easy to pull the cart up directly behind then when you are done harnessing. Another option to consider, especially if your dog is nervous if you get too far away or they can't watch you the whole time, would be to place your dog in a 'Stay' with then facing towards the cart so you remain in their line of sight while you leave to get the harness. Figure out which works the best for you and use this technique each and every time.

"Once you have your dog harnessed, you can point them in the direction you want to go and bring the cart up behind them for the hitch. Alternatively, some people like to use a 'Step In' technique where the dog is brought up near the cart in the direction of the shafts, and they step between the shafts ready to be hitched without having to move the cart. For brace teams, it's common to get both dogs harnessed and standing side-by-side for the hitch, but I've also seen handlers stagger the placement of the dogs so that one dog is hitched and that dog then brings the cart up to the second dog for hitching. Again, experiment with different techniques, and find one that works best for you.

"If you get to the point where you are doing the Open class, your cart will be positioned near the ring entrance, but outside of the ring. In this case, you will not have to deal with Basic Control or Recall, but you cannot bring your dog with you outside of the ring, so you will have to rely on one of the variants of the 'Stay' technique while you leave to get your cart. Once you have your dog positioned, remove the leash and bring it with you, dropping it in the cart when you get there."

"None of this sounds particularly difficult," said Mike.

"In theory it's not. However, you will find it can be very intimidating to work through the complexities of getting a harness onto your dog very early in your performance, especially if your dog has a tendency to just want to get going. It is typically very quiet, and you will have two judges staring at you while you work, trying to ensure that you put the harness on correctly and that you get it hitched to the cart correctly. Remember that this is not a timed exercise, so stay calm, remember to breath, and just work slowly and methodically through the process. "No matter how carefully you position and place the harness into the cart, it always seems to be tangled once it comes out. Make sure you get all of the straps positioned correctly, remember to lift the dog's feet through a Siwash if that's what you're using, and remember to buckle all the buckles. When it comes to hitching, make sure your singletree or doubletree is in the correct position and is moving freely, and that your traces run directly from the tree or eyebolts to the rings on the harness without wrapping around the shafts in any way. Finally, always take a moment to work your hands around the harness and attachments making sure that nothing is pinching and that you haven't accidently gotten a bunch of fur caught in a buckle.

"If you are in the Novice class, your final piece of the exercise will be retrieving and reconnecting your leash to your dog's collar. This will signal the judge's that you are ready for inspection. In Open class, the leash will remain in your cart, so just acknowledge the judges when you are ready for inspection. Most BMDCA judges will not perform a hand's on examination, and typically the inspection is fairly cursory if they did not see anything being done incorrectly during the exercise. They will give you an 'Exercise Finished' when they have completed the inspection. If anything is found to be incorrect, but does not have the potential to effect the safety of the dog while pulling, you may still pass the exercise. If anything will effect the dog's safety, you will likely fail the exercise and be asked to make changes before proceeding with the Maneuvering portion of the test.

"If you ever try a Newfie test, you will bring your dog off-leash to a position twenty feet in front of your cart. You must leave your dog in a 'Stay' while you retrieve your harness from the cart. You will then harness your dog and back your dog towards the cart. You must go back at least four feet, but you have

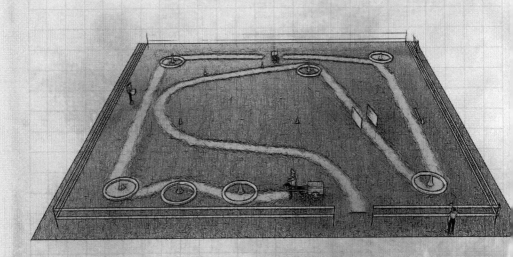

Weaves, Circles, 90-degree Turns and About Turns

the option to back all the way to the cart, or to bring the cart to the dog. Upon completing the hitch, you will be asked to move your rig forward while the judges inspect the equipment. At this point they will perform a fairly intensive hands-on inspection with both judges checking the harness and hitch for safety and efficiency. You will then proceed into the maneuvering portion of the test.

"For the Rottie test, you will harness your dog before you even approach the ring and once at the ring entrance, you hitch to the cart in a manner similar to the Berner test. Rather than proceeding directly into the maneuvering through, you will add your freight load of forty pounds and carry it along for the maneuvering portion of the test."

"So to make your harness and hitch a little bit more formal, let's set up a ring gate, I'll put your cart into position, and you can come into the ring and perform Basic Control and then Recall back to the cart. Once you've harnessed and hitched, I'll perform an inspection, and then you can start the rest of your practice session."

After a harness and hitch, and some warm-up, including pulling straight, veer turns, pivot turns, and halts, it was time to add in some more practice exercises.

"So what's next?" asked Mike.

"I want to show you a couple of more turning exercises that are not actually called out in the BMDCA rulebook, but that you may run across occasionally. These are weaves and figure eights. Both of these exercises will help you hone your turning skills, and if you do run across them, you'll already know what to do."

"If they aren't in the rule book, how do they get into the test?"

"Although the rule book spells out the minimum obstacles that must be included, judges are given the flexibility to design their course to take advantage of any naturally occurring obstacles, such as trees. If a nicely spaced row of trees presents itself, there's often a lot of temptation to use them. Besides you still need to get from point A to point B, and often it's difficult to simply work around all of the natural obstacles.

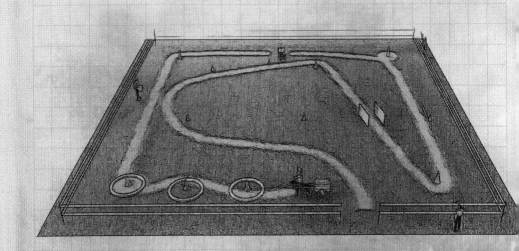

Weaves

Some judges, myself included, like to put a series of weaves early in the course design because it gives the handler and dog an opportunity to start working together before they get into the more technical obstacles. Often the last weave obstacle is used as a required 90-degree turn or circular pattern. Figure eights are convenient too if you find yourself having designed a course where it would be difficult to add circular patterns. If you head between two obstacles, a circle left followed by a circle right or vice-versa, results in a figure eight and takes two required elements off the list of required elements in a relatively small area.

"If you end up doing other breed tests, you will find that weaves and figure eights are also not specifically called out in the Newfie test, but they do stipulate that the maneuvering course includes as many natural terrain features as possible, so you might see them for the same reasons I described for a Berner test. The Rottie test specifically requires a weave or "serpentine" with a minimum of 5 pylons, nine feet apart as one of their mandatory exercises. In addition, they list a set of three optional exercises, which includes a figure eight. Of the three, the judge may select any two, so you have a pretty reasonable expectation that you'll see a figure eight in a Rottie test sooner rather than later."

"OK, but aren't these just nothing more than series of veers or pivots combined together?"

"You are correct. But don't assume that just because you can veer or pivot in an open field or even around a single obstacle, that this is the same thing as a series of turns in a defined area around multiple obstacles. While you already have the basic and advanced turning skills we've already been working on, we've never really talked about the most important part of an exercise like a weave or figure eight."

"And that is?"

"Having a plan. It sounds so simplistic, but I have to say that many handlers have unnecessary difficulty with these types of exercises because they did not know how to align themselves heading in and how to set up the subsequent obstacles to ensure success.

"Let's start with a weave and we'll assume that it's set up using traffic cones. I think a lot of handlers perceive this exercise to be a series of individual turns

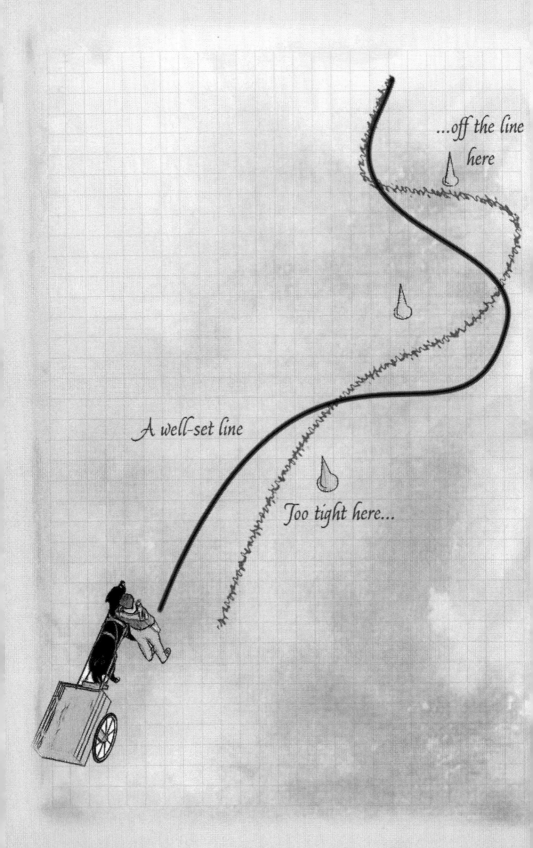

rather than the single flowing sequence that it really is. Because of this, they address the turn around the first traffic cone as if the rest of the turns aren't part of the same exercise. When they complete their first turn, they often find themselves badly out of position to execute the second turn, and so on down the line. Much of this is correctable during the middle of the exercise with that excellent pivot turn we've been working on, but if your dog has not progressed beyond a veer turn, then being out of position anywhere in the exercise can lead to not being able to recover. You either miss the next traffic cone in the row, or you have to circle out in the opposite direction to get back into the sequence.

"Without a plan, or what I like to call 'setting your line,' many handlers head from the previous obstacle directly at the first traffic cone. They pass close to the side of the first traffic cone, they then execute their turn which gets them around the first cone rather easily, but the radius of their turn puts them too far out of position to turn back and approach the second traffic cone. In reality, you want to head a few feet to the side of the first traffic cone, ideally with the distance being the radius of the turn you are about to execute. This way, your turn will pass neatly at the center of the distance between the first and second traffic cones, and this becomes the inflection point of your turn, or the location where you are no longer turning in the direction of the first turn and you start turning in the direction of the second turn. If you keep this in mind as you progress through the weave, you will have plenty of spacing and will not run the risk of accidentally colliding with any of the traffic cones. Widen the width of your "S" turn through the series to hit each center point between two cones correctly. Going into the series too flat against the cones can also lead to positioning issues, but also set you up for your cart accidentally hitting a traffic cone as you are setting up for the next one.

"As a general rule, regardless of the exercise you are performing, always remember to check your path in front of you, then check the location of your dog, then check the location of your cart, and adjust your maneuvers accordingly before repeating this pattern over and over. Many handers just check their own location or the location of the dog, and never look back to see the position of the cart relative to the obstacle. The difference between hitting and avoiding contact is often knowing where the cart is, and taking one additional step forward before executing your next maneuver."

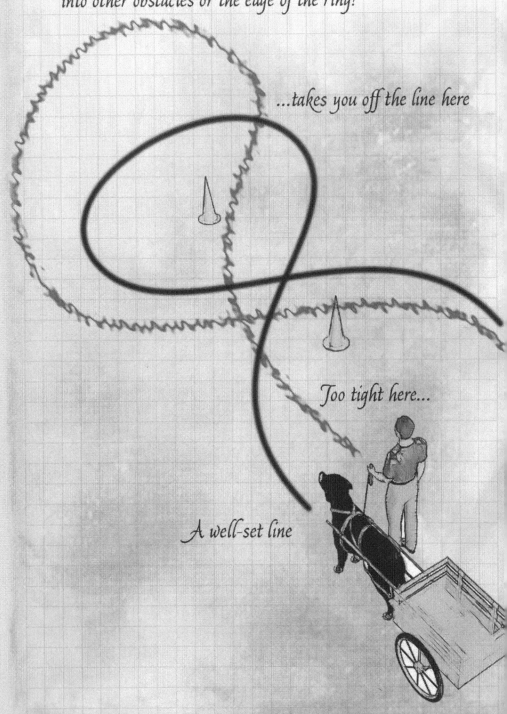

"I assume these concepts work for a figure eight as well?" asked Mike.

"Absolutely. It's the same principle. You want to head into the middle of the figure eight equidistant between the two traffic cones you will be circling, and you want to start your first turn just as you hit that mid-point. Circle too early, too late, or at a location not equidistant between the traffic cones, and you will typically pass around the first cone easily enough, but you will find yourself out of position for executing the second turn. If you find yourself in this circumstance, your correction is to try to get back to the midpoint between the cones heading straight into the obstacle before you start your second turn. As before, you'd be amazed as too how much poor planning or positioning you can correct for if you have a strong pivot turn at your disposal, but you have to remember to watch your cart behind you since these sharp turns often result in your cart getting very close to the item you are circling.

"Finally, when walking the course and setting your line between the previous obstacle and your next obstacle, keep in mind that the shortest distance between two points may not be the best or only option. You are not required to go directly from any one obstacle to the next along a straight line, but if you decide to change your course for the sake of better positioning or alignment, you must show teamwork and control in doing so. Aside from weaves and figure eights, it's always a good idea to extend these basic concepts to any pair of obstacles you need to negotiate. If you approach each exercise as independent from the next, you often don't put yourself in the best position to get to the subsequent obstacle. Always think about the ideal approach angle to the next obstacle after the one you are completing, and put yourself in the best position for success as you leave the current obstacle by thinking about the next one before you even approach it. This may also include switching the side of the dog you are working on to keep your body between your dog and an obstacle.

"Let's set up a few traffic cones for weaves and figure eights, and you can practice these concepts as you work from one exercise to the next."

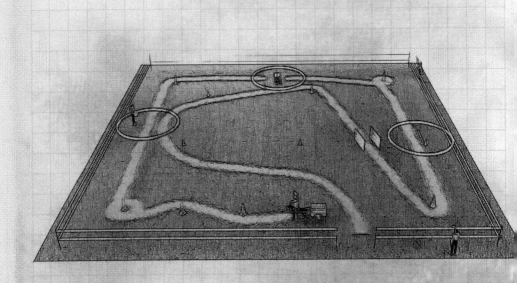

Halts and Waits

After a few runs through the weaves and the figure eights, I asked Mike to start switching sides, first to keep himself as the inside pivot point for all the turns, and then to try the same exercises again by putting himself on the outside of all of the turns.

"It really makes a difference on these turns as to which side you are standing on," said Mike. "It's almost as if Shogun doesn't want me standing on his left, and he tries to get around me and back into what he considers his normal heel position."

"That's just something you're going to have to work through, and one of the reasons it's important to start working both sides of your dog early. Ideally there should be no difference to you being inside or outside on both left and right turns. If you can build this into your toolkit, they you as the handler will always have the option of putting your body in the most advantageous location relative to your dog as you work through additional exercises.

"And speaking of working both sides of the dog, that leads us nicely into the next topic of building on the halts and waits you've already been working on. There are three exercises that we'll work through that will test the quality of your halts and waits – 'loading,' 'unloading,' and the 'removable obstacle.' Each of these exercises is meant to simulate a real-world situation that you might encounter while drafting with your dog.

"First, let's take a look at the loading exercise. In this case, you will be drafting along and you will encounter a friendly stranger who will want to give or sell you something that you will need to place in your cart. Think of a farmer's market where you are navigating your way past various stalls of merchandise and you find something you want to bring home.

"The first thing the exercise requires is that you 'halt' your dog. Make sure you start your 'halt' far enough away from the friendly stranger you are about to encounter so that your dog does not make contact with them. As with any 'halt' throughout the draft test, you dog must execute the command willingly and on their own accord.

"If you move yourself around in front of the dog an act as an impediment to their progress, this is called 'body blocking,' and will typically result in a failure to 'halt' in whatever section of the exercises you are performing. As usual,

137

try not to put the judges in the position of having to interpret whether your movement in front of your dog was the reason that they stopped.

"You will be judged on your 'wait,' meaning you can set your dog into whatever position you want, be that standing, sitting, or lying down, and the dog can change position, from one to another, but he can't change location, meaning he cannot move to a new location while you are conducting the exercise. Next, you will signal the friendly stranger, typically a ring steward, and they will commence with greeting the handler. This is typically just a verbal, such as, 'Good morning,' or 'Hello,' but don't be surprised if the greeter attempts to shake your hand. Strictly speaking this isn't in the rulebook, but it is a common interpretation of 'greet the handler.'

"Then the greeter will hand you the load, which is usually a small, lightweight item that will fit in most carts. The load runs the gamut of possibilities and often matches the theme of the draft test. I have seen blankets, boots, pumpkins, duffle bags, and baskets full of smaller items. You will get a chance to see the load during the pre-test walkthrough, so make sure you determine that it will fit easily in your cart and if you will need to tie it down with bungie cords or a cargo net. Once you have received the load from the greeter, your job is to get it into the cart and secured if necessary. Once done, you return to your dog, retrieve your leash if you are using one, and the exercise is complete. You then release your dog from the 'wait,' and proceed to the next exercise carrying the load in the cart."

"Well, that doesn't sound too difficult," said Mike. "Other than having a solid 'halt,' what else do you need to know? And by the way, you started this whole description talking about working both sides of your dog – how does that fit in?"

"The skill is always in the details, and you've hit on one of them, which is which side of the dog do you want to work? We've discussed that there is a tendency for handlers to work in traditional heel position with the dog to the left of the handler. As you approach the loading exercise, you may wish to keep yourself between your dog and the greeter, which means you need to be comfortable working both sides of the dog, and switching from one to the other as needed.

Nothing wrong with setting up from a traditional "Heel" position, but...

Being between the dog and the greeter may allow you better control of the exercise

"If your dog is particularly friendly to strangers, there may be a lot of temptation for the dog to try to approach the greeter. Keeping yourself between the greeter and your dog gives you distance and time to work.

"Once you are halted, you will want to place your dog into whichever position you deem to be the most reliable. For me, this is always putting the dog into a down stay because it takes the most effort for your dog to break out of a down stay in order to move towards the greeter. That said, many handlers have success using a stand stay or a sit stay. Do what works for you, be consistent across all of these exercises in whichever position you use, and try not to settle for allowing your dog to dictate which type of stay they are willing to give you. In cases where the dog 'forgets' the words 'sit' or 'down,' handlers often give up and leave the dog in an unpracticed stand stay. When they turn to move, the dog comes with them. Try to spend the extra time to get the dog into your desired position before commencing with the rest of the sequence. Occasionally a handler positions their dog and simply turns away without a command to commence with the sequence, and their dog follows them as they move to the greeter or turn to drop the load into the cart, so remember to actually issue a command for your dog to 'wait,' using whatever command you like.

"The next thing to remember is that you control the timing of the exercise. The greeter will remain stationary until you acknowledge them to proceed with the sequence, so make sure both you and your dog are positioned the way you want before you feel obliged to proceed. Then, once the greeting is completed, be aware of the load, how you receive it, and what you do with it. Personally, I never want to pass the load over the head of my dog. A test is a potentially stressful situation, and your dog may react to the load item in an unpredictable way, not to mention that the load could fall and land on your dog. Don't give your dog the excuse to break their 'wait.' When I take the load, I always keep my body positioned between the load and my dog and I turn away from my dog so that for the most part, they never see the load item. I then drop it into the basket of the cart, attach it if necessary, and get back to heel position to complete the exercise.

"Bear in mind that the rule book states the judge's commands as 'halt,' 'load your draft rig,' and 'forward' for this exercise. I will tell you that there does not

seem to be a lot of consistency here. Sometimes the 'halt' is left to the handler's discretion and sometimes the judge asks for it. Beyond that, the running of the exercise is usually left to the handler, and it is often ended with, 'exercise finished' once the handler returns to heel position and is ready to proceed. I think this mainly is done to signify that the 'wait' is no longer being judged. Occasionally, no end command is issued and again the handler is left to proceed once they are ready. Ask about the sequence of commands during the walkthrough or watch a couple of maneuvering performances to see how the exercise is really being called.

"Finally, remember that there is no limit to the commands you can issue for this exercise, so you can ask your dog to 'stay' or 'wait' or anything else you want as often as you want. This is often helpful if you find your dog 'popping up' in anticipation of moving forward as you return to heel position. Remember that this is not an immediate fail, but if the dog pops up and starts moving, you have failed the 'wait' that is being judged. A couple of extra verbal commands or hand signals to hold position can be the difference between passing and failing."

"Okay, that is a lot of little details I wouldn't have thought of," said Mike. "Is the unloading exercise just the same thing in reverse?"

"For the unloading, there is an added component that results in another decision by the handler as to how they will control their exercise. Seldom are the loading and unloading exercises back-to-back, so you will have some other exercises to complete before the unloading. You will approach the unloading exercise similarly to the loading exercise in that you will execute a halt, execute a command to position your dog, and ask for a 'wait,' before you acknowledge the greeter and continue with the sequence. In this case, in addition to greeting the handler, the greeter will ask for permission to pat your dog. Make sure your dog is in a reliable position, make sure you are truly ready to proceed, and remember that again you can continue to issue commands throughout the sequence.

"The greeter will approach your dog and typically give it two or three light taps on the head before returning to their original position. The dog can't change location and can't show aggressiveness or shyness towards the greeter. In addition to this, you will also need to retrieve the load from your cart and

The Load will be less interesting if you keep it largely out of sight!

Passing the Load over or near your dog's head might be scary or a temptation!

return it to the greeter. The handler sets the order of these elements, so do it in a way that works best for you. My personal recommendation is the following sequence: first, I set the dog's position and issue the 'wait,' then I retrieve the load and hold on to it keeping it as far away from my dog as possible, then I acknowledge the greeter and ask them to pat my dog, and finally once they have returned to their starting position, I hand them the load.

"My reasoning for this is that my dog should be under the least stress and therefore most reliable in their wait while I retrieve the load before I get the greeter involved. By not returning the load immediately, the greeter approaches my dog empty-handed, preventing the opportunity for the steward to make a mistake by getting the load near my dog or accidentally dropping it. Finally, once they have returned to their start position, they are the farthest away from the dog, and I can hand them the load as I re-approach my dog, ensuring that my dog never really sees the load item."

"That seems like a lot of work to keep the load away from the dog," said Mike. "Are you really that worried about it? I seldom see your dogs pay any interest to anything while they are working."

"This is true, but why even take the chance? I've seen handlers and stewards drop items, I've seen loads passed over the dog's head or their back from the opposite side of the cart, and I've seen dogs suddenly take interest in the load or the greeter or both. I think my dogs would continue to work under most of these circumstances, but this is a chance to take variability out of the equation, so I do that consistently and repeatedly. For training purposes, you will want to try to work with a wide variety of greeters, so while you practice in your local park, try to ask for volunteers including both men and women, kids, and any variety of clothing and accessories you can find. Even people holding other dogs makes for an excellent challenge for your halts and waits, and this certainly ups the level of difficulty of you or your wife acting as the greeter while you practice in your driveway at home.

"As to tests for other breeds, they each treat the loading and unloading concepts quite a bit differently. For Newfie's, you will not have a load or unload exercise as part of your maneuvering course. However, as part of the group exercises, you will complete your three-minute stay, and then individually, each handler loads their cart for the freight haul with 25 to 100 pounds 'as appropriate,'

while the judges review and then inspect the loading for balance, safety, and appropriateness for the dog, rig, and conditions. At the end of the freight haul, and with the judges' permission, you will be asked to unload before unhitching your dog. For the Rottie test, you will load 40 pounds into the cart after the harnessing/hitching exercise, and you will perform all of the maneuvering with this weight in the cart. After completing the maneuvering course, you will unload the weights prior to commencing with the group down stay.

"Now, let's set up a loading and an unloading station. I'll act as the greeter and you can start practicing everything we've just discussed. First, we'll align the exercises so that you approach each station with yourself in heel position between Shogun and the greeter. Next, we'll reverse the stations so that you are approaching with Shogun between yourself and the greeter so you can see how you would adjust if you find yourself on the 'off' side of the dog. And finally, keep the stations the same and I'll have you move to the opposite of your normal heel position so that you can perform these in the mirror image of how you did the first set, again keeping yourself between Shogun and the greeter."

After about 20 minutes of greeting, loading, and unloading, it was time to move on.

"I really do feel more in control of the loading and unloading when I'm between Shogun and the greeter," said Mike. "There is definitely far less opportunity for things to go wrong."

"I'm glad you are finding the techniques helpful. Now, the final halt and wait exercise for today is the 'removable obstacle.' This exercise is meant to simulate moving through an area where there is something in your way, and you don't really have the option of going around it. The best example would be a gate in the middle of a fence or a hedgerow, but in other cases, the obstacle could be a wagon, bicycle, child's toy, or a tree branch sitting in the middle of the path you are on, and for whatever reason, you can't easily leave the path.

"The exercise calls for a 'halt' prior to the removable obstacle, and your dog must 'wait' while you address the obstacle. Once the path is cleared, the hander returns to the dog and proceeds. Depending upon the judges' discretion, and sometimes depending upon the nature of the obstacle, the handler may be required to return the obstacle to its original location. Often, gates are returned to the original closed condition while items lying in a pathway are not, but figuring equally into the equation is the number of teams participating in the test, weather conditions, and the amount of daylight available. Check with the judges during the walkthrough to determine whether you are required to return the obstacle. If so, once you have moved it, returned to your dog, and moved past the obstacle, you will repeat the 'halt' and the 'wait,' then you will reset the obstacle and return to your dog before proceeding.

"Since this exercise is considered part of the 'maneuvering' exercises, there are no specific commands associated with it. However, as with the loading and unloading, you may see some inconsistency as to whether the judge will call for the halt or just expect the handler to execute one in order to negotiate the obstacle. And in some cases you will get an 'exercise finished' to denote that the 'wait' is no longer being judged and that you may proceed.

"In terms of your handling, you want to approach the obstacle closely enough to convince the judges that you are in control and that your dog is not afraid of the obstacle. However, you do want to leave enough space to complete a good halt and to be far enough away that your dog cannot contact the obstacle while moving or during their 'wait.'

"Again, if you are experiencing pop-ups or Shogun starts moving forward once you clear the obstacle, remember that you can again use multiple and repeated commands for this exercise. For training purposes, it is common to treat your dog when you re-approach them after the wait. This can actually help lead to this pop-up behavior since you have just reinforced the concept that they have successfully completed the exercise. In order to prevent this or to break them out of this bad habit, only treat on a random basis, meaning you will re-approach and leave on irregular intervals, treating occasionally throughout, but trying to reinforce that the 'wait' should continue until told otherwise, and trying not to signal that a single return to your dog is always the end of the exercise.

"Again, tests for other breeds deal with similar concepts. The Newfie test calls for a removable obstacle, which is identical to what I've described for the Berners except their rules specify that the object must be returned to its original position. In the tests I've done, the obstacle has been a series of traffic cones that get stacked, then you move your team though before returning and un-stacking the cones. For the Rottie test, they specifically call for a 'Gate' with a four foot-wide opening.

"So now, in addition to the traffic cones for weaves and figure eights, we'll put my cart in the middle of the path, and I'll act as the load and unload steward, and we'll see if you can start putting together all of these exercises in various sequences."

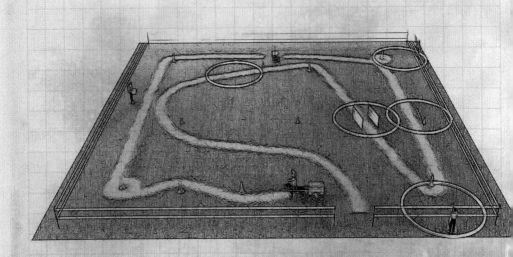

Distractions, Slows, Narrows and Backs

Distractions, Slows, Narrows, and Backs

The following weekend, we were back at our favorite park, and Mike and Shogun were navigating smoothly through ever more complex sets of turns. It was time to up the ante again.

"The next things I want to add to your practice are distractions."

Mike replied, "I thought the whole point of working here in the park was that we already have a higher level of distractions than I have when we practice at home."

"This is very true. We talked about the fact that similar experiences in different environments create different context for you dog, so you need to proof your commands and exercise through a variety of different locations and circumstances to know that you will be solid regardless of what you encounter. As far as a BMDCA Draft Test is concerned, you will need to deal with both naturally-occurring distractions, as well as specific auditory and visual distractions that are included as part of the maneuvering course. While the test is primarily concerned about your performance in the distraction exercises during the maneuvering course, you can fail outside of these specific exercises if your dog gives a failing performance in reaction to a naturally occurring distraction.

"Before we further distinguish naturally occurring distractions from those set up for the maneuvering course, let's discuss what constitutes a failing performance for distractions. The section of the rules is called 'Control with

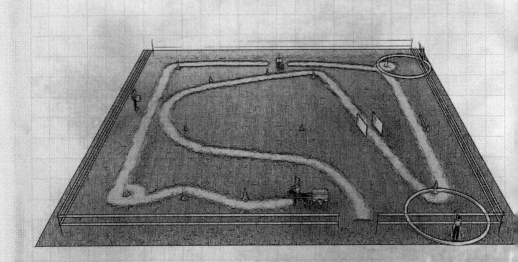

Audio and Visual Distractions

Distractions,' and this pretty well sums up the intent. Your dog is allowed to stop what it is doing and watch a distraction but it cannot divert from the course it was following, and it may not move the draft rig if the rig is at that moment stationary. So, if your dog changes direction in response to a distraction, moves a stationary rig in response to a distraction, chases the distraction, is fearful of or shows aggressions to the distraction, or refuses to resume the exercise it was performing after the distraction is gone, all of these would constitute a failure.

"The maneuvering course will have separate auditory and visual distractions somewhere in the course, approximately 10 feet from where the dog is working. Typically, stewards, under instructions from the judges as to when and how long the distraction should occur, control the distractions. Often the distractions are simple everyday items, and these can match the theme of the test.

"For auditory distractions, bells and whistles are common, as are sounds from squeaky toys or child's toys. I've seen metal food bowls used where the sound is the pouring of kibble from one to the other. I know some judges believe that this may be too much temptation and won't use this, but you can consider this a worst-case if your dog is very food-oriented, so I would suggest we practice for this.

"For visual distraction, you will see flags or towels being waved, umbrellas opened or closed, dog toys being tossed or pulled on strings, and possibly even another dog on a leash. Depending upon your dog's prey drive or friendliness, these types of distractions can be fairly difficult to overcome.

"Since the Draft Tests are often performed in public parks, you will need to be able to deal with other random distractions that occur either inside or outside of the ring. Squirrels can be a problem for many dogs. You may encounter joggers, skaters, bikers, or horseback riders around the ring area. Occasionally a person will try to cut through the ring instead of going around. Sometimes a small child will just wander under the ring ropes. And more than few times, a ball or Frisbee from a nearby field has rolled into the ring. While there is no controlling the distraction, your dog is expected to work through these situations just as if these were the scripted distractions for the maneuvering course.

Eye contact, verbal commands, hand signals, and proper positioning can make distractions disappear!

"Often, the distractions do not occur in isolation. They cannot be combined with other exercises that require judge's commands. Instead, they are performed in combination with other obstacles, most commonly turns. For example, let's say you are heading in a straight line towards a corner and you will be performing a 90 degree left turn or a left circular pattern. The distraction may occur as you head into the obstacle so that it is easy to distinguish whether the dog proceeds straight towards the distraction or executes the turn or circle as designed. If you are circling, make sure you know whether the distraction will occur the first time you pass the steward or the second."

"So what are the skills we need to train to deal with all of this?" asked Mike.

"You should hopefully already have what you need from your puppy training classes: the 'Leave It' command. Of course, you also have that toolkit of intangibles we've been building. As you head into the area where the distraction will be, I like to reinforce the commands I'm already executing. If we are turning, I give multiple 'Left turn, left turn,' commands and hand signals. This does a couple of things. First off, your commands can cover over the noise of auditory distractions and your hand signals can break the dog's field of view so that they cannot establish eye contact with visual distractions. Next, if you are concerned that your dog has acknowledged a distraction, you can give immediate 'Leave It' commands and repeat that as often as needed. I'd immediately follow this up with a reissue of the original command, such as 'Left turn,' again.

"In terms of training, if you've never used the 'Leave It' command before, this is pretty simple. You issue the command 'Leave It' as the dog's attention turns to something other than you, and treat as soon as their attention returns to you. As usual, you are reinforcing a behavior where you make yourself the most interesting thing to your dog. Eventually, you will wean down the immediate treats for the proper execution of 'Leave It,' since you may not always have a treat handy when a situation presents itself, but always be sure to praise your dog for the proper execution of this command.

"You also have your intangibles, so work through these and find the ones that work best for you in distraction situations. Often a handclap, or a couple pats on you leg are enough, or you may find these to be good situations for a

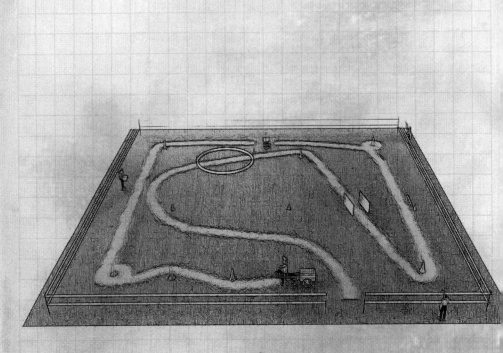

Slow

continuous running dialog – whatever it takes to keep their attention. Finally, this also a good time to analyze the setup of the exercise and to determine which side of the dog you should be working on to keep yourself between your dog and the distraction. For the most part, if you never let them see it or hear it, then the distraction is not much to deal with.

"For the Newfie test, you will find rules for 'intriguing' distraction that occurs naturally as either part of the maneuvering or the freight haul course. For the Rottie test, one distraction is listed as one of the defined course elements. Neither of these tests distinguishes between primarily auditory or visual like the Berner test, so again, be prepared for either or a combination of the two. Let's get a course set up, and you can repeat the exercises you've already been working on, and I'll add in a couple of distractions, first at locations you are aware of, and later, I'll just randomly add them in as you are working."

"Sounds good," said Mike. "I'm eager to see how much additional proofing were going to need to add to exercises that I thought were pretty solid already."

"Well that went better than I expected," said Mike. "I like your suggestion about using the various techniques to effectively prevent Shogun from even knowing there is a distraction."

"Well, very few drafting problems can't ultimately be solved if your dog is actually paying attention to you. I think it's time to move on to our next exercise, specifically, the 'Slow.' You've probably found yourself already at least asking for this behavior, if you're not already training for it outright. While some dogs are just naturally slow and steady while they work, others tend to get pulling and decide that you should keep up with them, instead of the other way around. In any case, much like a good pivot turn, you will want a reliable slow in your bag of tricks, even if you are not actually using it for the specific 'Slow' exercise. 'Slow' is often used when setting up turns or aligning yourself for other obstacles, and it is invaluable if you like to work both sides of you dog because you can cross in front of your dog while they are slowing and get to the other side instead of having to use a halt.

In addition to all other signals, changing your posture can indicate to your dog the need for a change of pace!

"In terms of training, as with everything else, shape the behavior you want using your treats, and when you are getting it consistently, start adding your voice or hand signals. In the case of a slow, you will want to get your dog up to speed, and then you can drop a treat down in front of their nose and pull it towards you so that you have them looking at you for visual queues. At this same time, you will want to slow your pace substantially. This often works well if you accompany this with a change of posture. For example, if you typically take long strides and are leaning somewhat forward as you go, you can shorten your stride down to heel-toe, and get very vertical in your stance. Your dog can key off of all of these visual clues in addition to the commands you add to the sequence. If your dog slows in response to the sequence, give them the treat and continue to treat for the length of the slow.

"Just as important, make sure you take time to train the exit of the slow, which is your return to normal pace. Change your posture back to what you had preceding the slow, and issue a command or signal to get them back up to speed. If necessary, use your treats here in front of the dog's nose and move it out briskly in front of them so that they have to catch up to you to get it. During the exercise, the judge will call for 'Slow' and later, 'Normal.' Only the actions are being judged, not the commands, so while I do use 'Slow,' I break back to normal pace with 'Let's Go!' All of the rest of your intangibles are available to you, so try whatever you need to get your dog's attention as you go into and out of the slow."

"I have been asking for him to move slower at certain times, but I never really thought about specifically training for this." Mike continued, "I guess it only makes sense. I always forget that he doesn't really understand something until I train them him to do it."

"We'll add this to your practice sessions and he should start showing improvements right away. Now, in terms of actually doing this as a draft test exercise, there are several things to keep in mind. First, the 'Slow' must be for a minimum of ten feet. Second, the judge is looking for the dog to execute a 'Slow.' If the handler slows, but the dog does not, this will result in a failure of the exercise. Also, while you know about where the 'Slow' will occur, the judge will call for 'Slow' and then you can execute your command. Don't anticipate the judge's call either for 'Slow' or for 'Normal.' In fact, if it feels like the judge

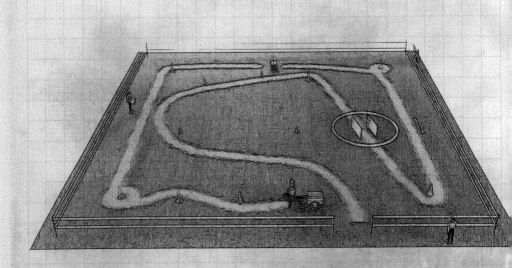

Narrows

is taking quite a while to give you the 'Normal' command, it is probably a pretty good indicator that they haven't yet seen the required ten feet of slow. Depending upon the course arrangement, they may let you continue for a bit, or they may call 'Normal' without ever having seen the 'Slow' in the first place.

"In the BMDCA rulebook, the definition of 'Slow' is a pace distinctly different and slower than the pace immediately preceding, and followed by a return to the preceding pace. Because of this definition, you will sometimes hear the exercise called the 'Change of Pace.' Some handlers use this to their advantage if they have especially slow-working dogs. In essence, they ask their dog to speed up in preparation for the 'Slow,' then the execute the 'Slow' by issuing their command and returning the dog it its standard slower pace. They then speed up to demonstrate 'Normal' before eventually letting the dog naturally slow back to their standard slower speed. Several judges I've spoken to do not like this approach, but unless the definition of 'Slow' is changed to include wording about the dog's normal pace, it is perfectly allowable to use this approach.

"Whichever way you choose to approach the exercise, make sure you show a definitive change of pace both into and out of the 'Slow.' Both the Newfie and Rottie tests require a 'Slow' as one of the maneuvering course elements, but neither defines the 'Slow' to the degree found in the BMDCA rulebook. You should find yourself successful in any of these tests with the techniques I've just outlined."

"Sounds good," said Mike. "Let's set up a designated area and we'll give this 'Slow' a try."

"Now that you have a good start on a solid 'Slow,' you will probably need it to set up for the next exercise, the Narrows. This exercise is meant to mimic working through any confined space, or a tight opening such as a gap in a hedgerow, or across a footbridge over a stream. One thing to keep in mind is that the exercise is somewhat stylized, but it is meant to simulate a situation where you can't easily just go around without either climbing over the hedge or getting your feet wet.

Dog & Cart perfectly aligned on the narrows!

"In order to meet this goal, the handler, the dog, and the cart all must pass through the Narrows without making contact with it. The arrangement for a 'narrow area' is two parallel items, typically fences, two to four feet high and two to four feet long, set twelve inches wider than the widest part of your draft rig or the hitched dogs.

"So in order to pass the exercise," said Mike, "I need to lead Shogun through the Narrows with six inches on either side of the cart?"

"Well, most handlers will lead their dog through the Narrows, but you will also see an occasional handler set their dog's alignment to the Narrows and then they will just move themselves immediately behind the cart and follow the dog through. You could technically walk beside the cart, but there is so little room in the Narrows that I've never seen anyone try this technique. As to six inches on either side, well this would be ideal, but you will often see eleven and a half on one side and one half on the other. You don't have to be perfect, but cutting it that close is a good way to take years off a judge's life, not to mention the spectators. Ironically, most of the time the handler never really gets a good look at just how close they really are to having their cart hit."

"Why is that?"

"Well, the handler is typically moving and often trying to turn to set up for the next exercise. I will caution you against setting up for the next exercise too early. The key to success for this exercise is remembering that you, your dog, and your cart all have to go through without hitting. If you are leading your dog, you need to remember that your dog is trailing you and the cart is trailing a few feet behind your dog.

"Don't stop working through this exercise until you are sure that your cart is all the way out. I can't tell you the number of times that someone has failed because they make a last second move to step left or right or to turn around, and their dog dutifully follows them resulting in the cart nicking the end of the narrows just before the cart fully exits. Most course designs, even the ones that look a little tight from a maneuvering perspective, will leave you enough room to get fully out of the Narrows before you need to start positioning for something else."

"What other types of problems do you typically see?" asked Mike.

"We've just discussed issues with exiting the Narrows but I would say most of the problems occur before the team ever enters the Narrows. Specifically, I see alignment issues, or the handler's perception of alignment issues. These are typically the result of not setting a good line from the previous obstacle or exercise to the Narrows. In the case of this exercise, you will want your alignment to center your dog and cart into the entrance of the Narrows, which means that if you are handling from heel position, you as the handler will typically need to aim yourself in such a way that you would be passing just to the outside of the "Narrows.' Using your good 'Slow' technique can help give you more time to tweak your alignment as you approach the exercise. Once you have done your preliminary alignment, the handler typically halts their dog a couple of feet from the entrance to the Narrows, and then they move around in front of their dog to check their alignment by determining the amount of space they see on each side of the cart. If the alignment is not good enough, you can try to realign right at the entrance by giving your dog a 'Side Step' or 'Pivot' command if you have these in your tool kit. If not, you can elect to circle to realign.

"As long as your dog is cooperating, you will generally not be penalized for electing to circle. If you do elect to circle, try not to get flustered, take a moment to plan out your strategy, and don't execute it in a panic. Without a plan, this often results in a circle left or right that puts the dog exactly back in the same position as the one that you thought was not a good alignment in the first place. With a solid strategy, you will use the layout of the ring and any nearby obstacles to move yourself out far enough to ensure that you can get a better alignment the next time."

"How many times can you circle if you don't like your alignment," asked Mike?

"Well, there is no specific rule on this, so as long as your dog is cooperating, you can probably get away with a couple of circles. However, at a certain point, if the judges don't determine that you lack the teamwork to get aligned to execute the Narrows, your dog may get frustrated with all of the circling and become less and less responsive, or may elect to try the Narrows with or without you. After all, they see the Narrows in front of them and understand the general concept, but they don't understand why you are not letting them perform the exercise. My advice on this is to actually practice misalignment

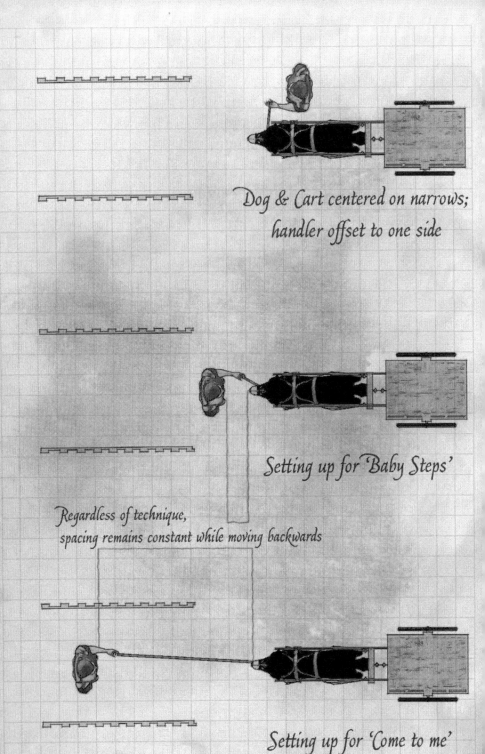

and determine the amount of correction that you can do either at the entrance or by executing slight steering adjustments commands within the Narrows itself. Essentially, at some point, you need to know that good enough is good enough on your alignment and that you can still get through. You may be best served just trying to get through the obstacle rather than circling again.

"Another issue can be where the handler elects to halt their dog. If you let your dog get too far forward into the entrance of the Narrows, you run the risk of the dog being able to sniff or contact the Narrows with their nose. This also makes it difficult, if not impossible, to get around in front of your dog to get yourself through the Narrows. A pivot turn might get you out of this, or you may need to try to back them up, but we'll discuss that later. I used to try to get my dog to halt with just enough space for me to sneak in front and into the Narrows. I'd say my newer philosophy on this is to halt quite a bit further back from the entrance of the Narrows, perhaps as much as four to six feet. This leaves me plenty of space to get my 'Halt' completed, more room to get around in front, and the longer distance to the entrance allows me a little more distance to make last minute corrections without the alignment having to be quite as perfect. Also, if I elect to circle, I have more room to get my turn executed without accidentally hitting anything."

"OK, so assuming I get my alignment good enough," said Mike, "how do I actually bring Shogun through the Narrows?"

"There are a couple of schools of thought on this. The first technique is what I call 'Baby Steps.' Essentially, you complete your alignment, halt your dog, and then your cross in front of your dog and you reverse your position so you are backing yourself through the Narrows. You will get in front of your dog in close proximity so that your dog can only take about one or two steps at a time. Then moving slowly and asking you take a step back and ask your dog to come to you with a single step. Then you check your alignment, correct slightly from side-to-side as needed, and repeat until you proceed fully through and out the other side. This technique works well if you have a slow-working, steady, reliable dog who won't get frustrated with the slow pace and repeated commands.

"A technique I am seeing more and more often is what I call 'Come to Me.' This relies on your dog's obedience skills to come forward directly to wherever

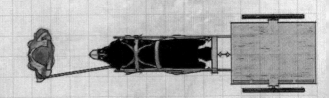

Setting up for leading the dog through the narrows

Setting up for trailing the dog through the narrows

you are standing. After aligning and halting your dog, you move through the Narrows until you are four to six feet away from your dog, then you turn to face them. On command, typically 'Here,' or 'Come to Me,' your dog moves forward and ideally straight to wherever you are standing. Since you are almost out of the Narrows, you can use the extra distance to make subtle steering corrections by sidestepping only a couple of inches to either side. As soon as your dog starts moving forward, you need to begin moving backwards at an equal speed. You can continue to call and steer your dog as needed, but remember to keep moving backwards until your dog and cart have cleared the exit of the Narrows. I find this to be an excellent technique for dogs with good obedience skills, who are also faster workers.

"One problem that can occur with faster workers, especially with the 'Baby Steps' technique, is that the dog understands the goal of getting out of the Narrows and actually attempts to pass the handler in order to do this. As you would expect, a collision occurs either with the dog to the handler, or the cart to the Narrows as the pass is attempted. The 'Come to Me' technique is an excellent way to avoid this. I've also seen a third technique, which is a 'Hybrid' of the other two. Basically the set-up is identical to the 'Baby Steps' technique, but the 'Hybrid' borrows the speed of movement and adjustments from the 'Come to Me' technique. Essentially, once you give your command for your dog to move, you stay just one step ahead of them but back quickly through the Narrows, correcting as you go. Since you are closer to the dog, I don't think you get as good of a view for corrections as you get with the 'Come to Me' technique, but this is something you can try for a dog that likes to work faster, but is not as good with the distance away from the handler and prefers being up close and personal.

"Other techniques include simply leading your dog through with the handler facing forward through the Narrows. This technique leans heavily on the quality of your initial alignment since you typically cannot see behind you to correct, and you must rely on your dog to follow you through on a straight line. And I had previously mentioned trailing your dog through, which again relies on the quality of your initial alignment. For this technique, if you plan to do any steering while in the Narrows, you will need to practice minor left and right correction from behind your dog using only voice commands.

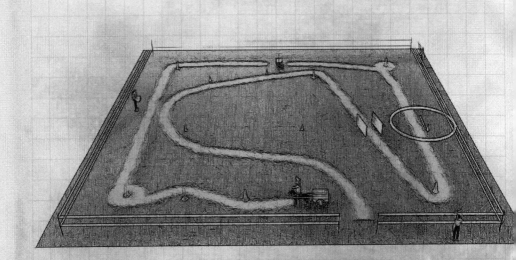

The Back Exercise

"For the other breed tests, the Newfies use two Narrows, both at least six feet long. One is typically a 'High Narrows' with solid sides, such as two parallel four foot by eight foot sheets of plywood, and one is typically a 'Low Narrows,' such as two parallel logs or two by fours. One of these Narrows should be adjusted to twelve inches wider than the widest part of the dog and apparatus and the other must be at least eighteen inches wider than the widest team/apparatus entered. The Rotties include a 'Bridge' obstacle as one of their three optional course exercises. Since each course must include two of the three optional exercises, you have a pretty good chance of encountering the 'Bridge.'

"I think it's time to get a couple of Narrows set up for you to practice with. Some people build their own Narrows for practice using wood or PVC pipe. If you don't want to build, a pair of soft crate set up next to one another makes an excellent set of Narrows. You can also look for naturally occurring Narrows throughout your training areas, for example, picnic tables can be set up side by side to make a long Narrows, or you can train on bicycle paths or foot bridges to provide a similar experience.

"The final technique you will want in your tool kit is backing. While you will ultimately need to prepare for a 'Back' exercise, the ability to back, much like the pivot turn, will get you out of just about any tight spot you get yourself into. In general for your dog may not be familiar with backing up without the cart, let alone with it. Depending upon what we see here today, you may need to work on backing at home before you proceed to trying this with the cart.

"Backing is best taught in confined areas where the dog's natural tendency to want to turn around is limited. For this reason, many people will teach backing inside their house using a narrow hallway, the space between a couch and a coffee table, or the space between a bed and a wall, but it is easiest if you have access to both an entrance and an exit in your set up.

"Guide your dog into position by luring them with treats into the exit where the dog will ultimately back out and all the way to the entrance where they will start the exercise. Use your treats to push the dog backwards. While some people will train by pushing the treat back over the dog's head, I find there is too great a tendency for the dog to want to sit when this occurs. Instead, I prefer to push the treat past the dogs nose and down under their chest. This makes them dip their head and raise their rear while they step backwards to

When training for backing, an assistant with a belly-strap can help prevent the dog's tendency to sit

get their head in position to get the treat under their chest. Continue to use additional treats under their chest and give them the treat only when they actually move backwards to receive it. Once your dog starts offering the back up behavior in order to get the treat, then you can start adding your verbal or hand signal commands. Your dog should be readily backing through the confined course using only a single treat at the end before you up the difficulty to a wider hallway or eventually backing in the middle of the room.

"Once your dog is capable of backing without the cart, then you can start reworking the behavior with the cart. As we've mentioned, the context of performing this exercise is considerably different with the cart in the equation, so don't be surprised if your dog will not back or will not use the command you've already trained. Be prepared to potentially use a different command or signal if needed, but you will essentially want to train the back the same way. With the dog harnessed and hitched and in a stand stay, use your treats by passing down past their nose and up and under their chest. Give the dog the treat initially for any backward movement, and then later for any backwards movement that results in the cart moving backwards as well.

"If your dog has a tendency to sit while backing, you can use a strap under the dog's belly to help work through eliminating this tendency. If you have an assistant, just wrap a strap or a leash under the dog's belly in front of their rear legs and have the assistant apply an upwards pressure as you work with your treats to get the dog moving backwards. If you don't have an assistant, you can do something similar by tying a strap or leash between the cart's shafts in order to accomplish the same thing."

"How much backing do I need to be able to do?" asked Mike.

"Ideally, you will want them to back on command for as long as you ask for the behavior. In terms of the Draft Test exercise, for Novice class you need to back one foot, and for Open class you need to back four feet. I would eventually try to get up to eight to ten feet as my minimum for practice.

"The exercise is timed, and you have sixty seconds to back the full-required distance. You will enter the prescribed backing area and the judge will generally ask you to 'Halt' your dog, although you are supposed to know that the 'Back' exercise will occur so you should be prepared to 'Halt' on your own

accord. You may have some limited options for placement around the backing area, so look to avoid uneven terrain. You may be faced with backing on a slight hill, so practice backing both uphill and downhill and if one of these is not as strong as the other, try to position yourself accordingly.

"Finally, the 'Back' exercise will be one of a sequence of exercises and obstacles, so make sure you know where you are heading next and determine if this will come into play for your positioning for the 'Back.'

"One thing to keep in mind if you are using a sled, toboggan or travois; since these devices are not designed for backing, you won't have to worry about it here. Instead you will perform your backup during the harness and hitch exercise. After harnessing your dog, you will back the required distance towards the cart into position to be hitched.

"Returning our focus to carts and wagons, once you've halted, you have the opportunity to position your dog and yourself for the exercise. Most people will have their dog back from a stand stay, but there are some who prefer to start from a sit or a down. Most handlers will reverse themselves and face their dogs for backing, but many handlers who also do Rally Obedience are now favoring a 'Rally Back' where you stand in heel position and you back along with your dog while facing forward. I'd suggest practicing for the 'Back' trying all of these techniques and settle on the ones that work best for you.

"The judge will ask 'Are you Ready?' As with any exercise that starts with this command, make sure you are actually ready before you acknowledge. Remember, in the case of a wagon, engage your locking pin mechanism before acknowledging your readiness. This is to prevent jackknifing while backing.

"As soon as you confirm you are ready, one judge will drop the measuring stick at the location of your cart wheel, and the judge calling the exercise will say, 'Back your dog,' and start the timer. Now is not the time you want to be adjusting yourself or your dog. The back must be substantially straight, and enough skewing to one side or the other can cause you to fail the exercise. Once you make it the required distance, or if time expires, the judge will call, 'Exercise Finished.'

"In addition, once the exercise starts with the 'Back your dog' command, any distance your dog moves forward, either on its own accord or in response to

you trying to straighten them out will be added to the distance you need to back to complete the exercise. In other words, wherever the measuring stick is lying is where you need to end up, so the one foot or four foot distance is not absolute. I've seen dogs back ten to twenty total feet during the exercise after moving forward or skewing, but they never make it to the location of the measuring stick and ultimately fail the exercise."

"Are there any tricks for this exercise?" asked Mike.

"The most common issue overall is that the dog seems to forget the understanding of the command 'Back.' They simply stand there behaving as if they've never heard the command before and they don't know what to do. As we discussed with other exercises, I'd invoke my 'Three Commands' rule here and then I'll try something else. If your dog doesn't respond to your requests to 'Back,' try another command, signal or technique that you've practiced before. For example, switch from a standard technique to a Rally technique or vice versa. If that still doesn't work, try any other command that might get the dog working again or starts some momentum to move the cart. For example, try a 'Sit.' In Novice, a single sit will likely get you anywhere from six to eight inches of distance, and more importantly may get your dog working. Follow this with a 'Stand,' and then 'Back' again. Sometime this will work, and sometimes it puts you in position to execute a second 'Sit.' If all else fails, try a 'Down' or even a 'Forward' command. You may add distance that you will need to back, but even a slight switch in their paw position or the location of the cart wheels may be enough to get your dog working and they might follow through with a 'Back.' The point is, asking for 'Back' for sixty straight seconds is most likely not going to get it done.

"Once your dog is backing, if they start to skew, you can in fact steer them, and I would recommend that this is something you practice. Often, if you are standing facing the dog directly in front, you will see that your dog has a natural tendency to skew to one side. Try offsetting yourself first to one side and then to the other while continuing to back. One direction will typically accentuate the skew and the other will typically diminish it or reverse it.

"Eventually you will learn where to position yourself to start and stay straight on the back, and this may not be directly in front of your dog. Then, if and when you need it, a slight side step to one side or the other will steer in reverse.

You can do similar techniques with a Rally back by changing the distance between yourself and your dog or changing the location of the had signal you use, either further left or right relative to the dog's head, depending upon what works best for you.

"Techniques to avoid include 'hovering,' which is where you are using your body to physically intimidate the dog to move backwards. This is usually seen when the handler's upper body leans way over the dog in an effort to get them to move backwards. Occasionally you will also see physical guidance to force the back as the handler's legs get closer to the dog to the point where contact is made and they actually force the dog back. Either of these will earn you a failure for the exercise even if the dog does eventually back the required distance.

"The Newfie test requires a three foot back while hitched to the cart within thirty seconds. I have often seen this positioned as a more practical demonstration of the need to back by first having the handler maneuver the dog into a tight spot up against a wall where there is literally no option except to back out. In addition, during the harness and hitch exercise, you start with the dog twenty feet in front of the cart. After harnessing, you are to back the dog to the cart for a minimum of at least four feet of backing. At that point you have the option of continuing to back the dog to the cart or leaving the dog in order to bring the cart to the dog. Rotties require a three foot back as part of their maneuvering course.

"Let's go ahead and try some backing without the cart, and we'll see if we're ready to start practicing this with the cart today, or if we'll wait for another session later once you have the basics down."

Legend was always the smart one. Long after her active drafting career was over, we found out that her sport was Rally Obedience, and she truly shined. We began to believe that Legend could actually read the signs on the Rally course, and to a large degree she seemed to understand them. Once at a

181

training demonstration, we loaned Legend to beginner handlers so they could try out a few exercises. After a couple of runs, one handler missed one of the exercises and headed off in another direction. Legend saw the sign for the exercise and sat and waited for the handler to return.

In retrospect, it should have come as no surprise that Legend would see the various obstacles on a draft course and would just know how to deal with them. She seemed especially fond of the Narrows, and if a run got anywhere close to the entrance of the Narrows, she would immediately head towards them and try to go through. You have to credit her for her enthusiasm, but unfortunately, this did not lead to good alignment heading into the Narrows, and often she would try to proceed through, with or without her handler. This led to some spectacular crashes during training, and my first realization that having a dog that was smarter than me was going to be a problem. It took us a couple of months to un-train this behavior. Lots of treats later we had finally convinced Legend to always look to her handler for instructions, even if she already knew the exercises.

Several years later, Watson presented us with yet another training problem at the Narrows. Watson also is convinced that he understands the exercise. However, while Legend was slow and steady, Watson moves through a draft course at a dizzying pace and a "look at me" strut to match. We could usually get Watson aligned to the entrance, but it was really difficult to get him to stop to allow his handler to lead him through the Narrows. Perhaps, in hindsight, Watson would have been a good candidate to allow the dog to lead through the Narrows and have his handler follow him. Fortunately, Watson was also a Rally dog, and had learned a nice Rally back, so if you could get beside him, you could usually work him back from the entrance enough to sneak through in front.

None of this proved to be much of an issue while Watson was pulling his cart alone, but when we added Smokey as his brace partner, we were again surprised by a new behavior. Smokey is another slow and steady worker, but he's utterly passive and was used to working brace with more type-A personality dogs, like his father, Marshall. In short, although he has a lot more drafting experience, Smokey defers all of the decision making to Watson.

We had just started competing in Open Brace a couple months earlier, and

hadn't really had any issues with the Narrows, so it was not really on my mental list of worries. We circled a hay bale and broke off at ninety degrees toward the entrance of the Narrows, over forty feet away. There was plenty of room to set up our alignment, except for one small thing – Watson forgot he was working as a brace team and decided that his definition of proper alignment was with him centered in the middle of the Narrows. The flaw to this plan with a thirty-six inch-wide brace cart was that it effectively placed Smokey outside of the Narrows, and would have split the cart in half had we proceeded. So we backed and we circled and we realigned and just as we approached the second time, Watson shifted to the center and Smokey blissfully allowed him to do it, and with a nice amount of momentum, we crashed into the Narrows. This was the only flaw in an otherwise excellent performance.

If you have the same dogs entered for multiple classes in the same day, it is not uncommon to pull from the group exercises to save the wear and tear of a half-mile with a one hundred ninety pound freight load. This theoretically leaves your dogs with more energy for their remaining events. In our case, my wife was going to show this same team in Novice Brace later in the day, and we decided that the last thing Watson needed was any more energy, so I went ahead and performed the Open freight haul, and when we were done we changed our strategy for the Narrows. We decided to halt the team several time during the alignment to the Narrows so that Watson would never have much momentum and would be unable to muscle Smokey out of his way. So after four halts and a long series of baby steps on the alignment into the Narrows, my wife got them aligned and through and then completed a passing Novice Brace performance.

Never be afraid to adjust your techniques on the fly if you encounter something that is not working for you. Remember Albert Einstein's definition of insanity: doing the same thing over and over again and expecting different results.

Group Exercises

Having worked through all of the individual exercises, it was now time to start focusing on the group exercises.

"So far, everything you've done has been just you and Shogun working as a team. We're going to change the context again, as we start working as a group. Even if you decide to never participate in competitions, these types of exercises are valuable because you'll often find yourself working around other dogs, and if you are in an area with working breeds that draft, you'll be working around other teams with carts as well. At the very least, we know your goal is 'Just a Walk in the Park' with my dogs and me, so you'll usually be drafting around my team anyway.

"When we start practicing, don't be surprised if your experience is a little rougher than you'd expect. If Shogun is in the front of the line with my dogs following, he may develop a tendency to try to look back over his shoulders to see what's following him, and he may halt occasionally to do this. If Shogun is following my dogs, he may develop a tendency to want to follow too closely, or to even try to pass because he's not yet used to holding a place in line. Don't worry though; we'll work through all of this."

"So everything we've learned so far is essentially going to have to be retested and tweaked again?" asked Mike.

"Absolutely. Things that were working perfectly before may now require you to go back to that toolkit of intangibles we discussed. Hopefully you don't have to

dig too deep to realize that every potential issue I've described will ultimately be solved by some variation of a technique to get Shogun refocused on you as the most important thing around, and it will all get solved from there.

"To start off, we'll just continue working with our maneuvering course that we already have set up. You'll run Shogun through the exercises as you've been doing before. The difference will be that I will have one of my dogs hitched up, and after we give you a head start, we'll start the same exercises in the same order. This is something that will never happen in an actual draft test because the maneuvering course is always run as an individual exercise. However, for our purposes, we need to make Shogun realize that other dogs may be working at the same time, and in any case, it ups the level of distractions, so you'll get to work harder at keeping him focused, especially in areas where our teams get close together. Use any technique you've got to get him refocused as the need arises. Let's get them hitched up and see how this works out."

"I never would have believed that something as simple as a turn could become so much more difficult," said Mike. "There were several times working through this that I wish I had been more attentive to where you and your dog were positioned, and there were quite a few times I wished that I had changed the side I was working from in order to help keep him more focused on me."

"Those are excellent observations. Independent of any possible competition, you never know what is going to cross you path or come up behind you while you are working, so you've got to be prepared at any moment for something completely unexpected, and you need to be able to find that perfect technique to get his attention back. And even if you are just working on that 'Walk in the Park,' you want to make sure you are working through a continuous cycle of looking in the direction you are going, looking down to check on your dog, and looking behind to check on your cart. This should help keep surprises to a minimum, and give you time to position yourself to your best advantage when you approach something, or something approaches you.

"Now that you've seen some of the practical changes that can occur when working in a group, let's discuss group exercises as they pertain to a BMDCA draft test. There are officially two group exercises, the 'Group Stay' and the 'Distance Freight Haul.' The groups are always separated by level, so Open will be grouped with Open, whether single or brace, and Novice will be groups with Novice, whether single or brace. No group can be larger than six teams, so the judges and the draft test secretary will determine where to break up the teams in order to meet these rules and to limit the number of group sessions as much as possible. Usually, the Open dogs complete first, followed by the Novice dogs, and often the brace teams compete within their groups before the single dogs; however, these are just tendencies and are not rules, so expect that the running order can vary from test to test, or even day to day at a multi-day test.

"After you have completed your individual work on the maneuvering course, you will exit the ring and then you can start getting prepared for your group exercises. If you are the first in your group to complete the maneuvering, you will have the longest wait before the group exercises, especially if the group contains the maximum of six teams. The last of the group to complete the maneuvering will have the shortest wait, but you will typically be given no less than five minutes to prepare, which is usually enough time to unhitch if you desire, get your dog some water and a quick potty break if needed, and then to load your freight haul weights and get re-hitched. Some people elect to keep their dog hitched while awaiting the group exercises, and if you elect to do so, you can try to find a shady comfortable place near the ring entrance to wait.

"When placing your freight load, make sure it is firmly attached and can't move around while you are working, and make sure it is properly balanced by gently checking the force exerted near the tips of the shafts. It's generally too late at this point to make major modifications, but if you know that your load should be balanced and it currently isn't, this can be an indicator that you loaded incorrectly or that something has shifted. If necessary, make any minor tweaks to ensure that the load is ready.

"While all of this is going on outside the ring, don't be surprised if there is action taking place inside the ring, even if all of the dogs within your group have completed their maneuvering. As test entries have gotten bigger in recent years, one technique for speeding up the overall test is something I call, 'Add-

a-Dog.' This means that instead of simply waiting five to ten minutes for the entire group to get ready, the judges proceed with the maneuvering portion of the test for the first dog in the next group. This will get them ahead of schedule while your group is hitching and loading. The judges or the secretary will typically inform the handlers that they will be using this technique during walkthrough session, so if you have any questions, make sure to ask your judges, and be ready to go into the ring when you are called.

"Teams will usually be asked to re-enter the ring in catalog order. You will typically follow a steward or a judge who will tell you where to position your team. This is often based upon available space in the maneuvering ring, as well as the direction of the sun. Often the arrangement is such that the sun will not be shining directly into the dog's eyes, and the arrangement will often take advantage of shade if there is any available. Once you are in the location they have requested, you can start positioning your dog for the 'Group Stay.' Since this is an actual 'Stay' that is being judged, your dog cannot change position or location."

"Is there any requirement for what position you put them in for the stay?" asked Mike.

"There is no required position in the rules, but since they cannot change position during the exercise, most handlers will put their dogs into a down stay, although a sit stay or stand stay are perfectly acceptable. I personally prefer the down stay since my dog actively has to work to get up, while it is far easier for a dog sitting or standing to decide that they prefer to be in a down partway through the exercise. The rules say that you may 'gently place' your dog in position. I see lots of handlers who do not realize this is allowed who try continually through verbal or hand signals to get their dog into position, often frustrating themselves and their dogs. Take advantage of the opportunity to gently assist your dog into position as necessary. The leash is then removed and is placed in the cart behind you.

"Once all of the dogs are in location, the judge will call, 'Position you dogs for the stay.' At this time, make any final adjustments; ensuring you like the position of your dog, and that there is nothing awkward going on with the harness, traces, or shafts that could make your dog uncomfortable. When all of the handlers are ready, the judge will call, 'Leave your dogs.' This exercise,

like the Novice Recall exercise, allows for only a single command in order to ask your dog to 'Stay.' As usual, the concept of 'Stay' is being judged, not your choice of command, so use whatever works best for you.

"Once you have issued your single command, then you will move forward to a location the judge designates. Novice handlers will then turn back to face their dog during the exercise for an in-sight stay, and Open handlers will be led out of the ring and behind some type of cover for an out-of-sight stay. For both classes, the stay is three minutes from the time the judge calls the 'Leave your dogs' command.

"Handlers should remain essentially as motionless as possible, and you will often see handlers with their arms crossed in front of them, or down by their sides. Do not make any sounds or perform any motions that could be interpreted by the judges as attempts to handle your dog from a distance. Minor movements from your dog are acceptable, such as adjusting their feet or rolling to the opposite hip, but they cannot change position or location. Occasionally a dog will move out of place, possibly approaching their handler or another dog. The judge will make the determination as to how to best handle this occurrence so that no other dogs are affected. This could include the judge or a steward approaching and holding onto the dog, or the judge asking the handler to hold onto their dog. Regardless of what occurs with someone else's dog, the expectation is that your dog will hold their 'Stay.'

"When the three minutes is over, Open handlers are guided back into the ring, and all handlers are asked to 'Return to your dogs.' You may approach directly back to the position you left and then spin one hundred eighty degrees to face the judges, or you may walk past your dog, around the back of the cart, and then forward into heel position. Regardless of what technique you prefer, expect a combination of both, and be aware that the judge will not call 'Exercise Finished' until all of the handlers are back in their original positions. At that time, you may talk to and praise your dogs, and if you are in the Novice class, you will reattach your leash for the freight haul. Open dogs will leave the ring off-leash for their freight haul."

"Are there any tips and tricks for the 'Group Stay?' asked Mike."

"As you can imagine, once you've started the 'Stay' portion of the exercise, your

performance will only be as good as the training you put into the exercise. Make sure you get your dog into the 'Stay' position you are surest of, and don't settle for another position because your dog suddenly realizes they don't understand the command you are giving. Practice your stays in many different environments, and with as many other draft dogs as possible. If you don't have any other teams to practice with, see if other people with dogs are willing to perform the exercise with you off-cart. In absence of that, other people or small children can make good stand-ins for other dogs. Arrange for distractions to occur during your practice stays. Anything that makes a noise or can move past or even through the practice area should be encouraged.

"As you train for your 'Stay,' be sure you work on increasing both time and distance over the course of a few sessions. Since you know you need three minutes, make sure you can get four or more during practice sessions. One of the most disappointing things that can occur is that your dog is perfect through the exercise until you re-approach, at which time your dog is so happy to see you that they pop-up and possibly even move towards you, either of which will be a failure for the exercise. In order to proof this portion of the exercise, vary the intervals at which you re-approach your dog from anywhere from thirty seconds to a couple of minutes, and when you do re-approach, either pass around behind the cart or spin at the heel position and leave your dog again. Repeating this randomness where you may or may not be ending the exercise will allow your dog to not try to predict when you are done. Do treat them as necessary to get this behavior. Initially you may need to treat each time you return to the dog. Eventually, wean them off the treats for every return and only treat once you have completed the exercise and are ready for them to move.

"Other tests use a similar arrangement for their group stays. The Newfies require you to bring your freight load to the location of their 'Three Minute Out-of-Sight' exercise, but you will perform the stay without the load, and you will load your cart as a separate exercise in preparation for the freight haul. The group is also no more than six teams, the stay is also three minutes, and you can use whatever position you prefer for your dog, but as the name says, it's always an out of site stay. The Rotties perform a 'Group Down Stay' with up to eight teams and no less than four feet between the carts, and they can combine different classes into a single stay if they wish. The group exercises may be

performed prior to the maneuvering or after all the maneuvering is completed at the club and judge's discretion. They stipulate that you must remove your armband, place it to the left of the cart, and weigh it down with your leash once it has been removed. As the name implies, this exercise must be done as a down stay, and it is an in-sight stay, also lasting for three minutes. The Berner and Rottie tests both stipulate the single 'Stay' command upon leaving your dog and they allow gentle guidance to position your dog. The Newfie rules are not as specific here, but using the single command is a safe bet for all three tests. In addition, the Newfie test states that the 'handler will instruct the dog to stay in a stand, sit or down position,' so be careful here not to physically guide your dog into position.

"From here, each test differs slightly. The Beners will already be loaded and ready for their freight haul. On the judge's command, you will follow the lead steward out of the ring, typically remaining in catalog order and available stewards will follow along to assist if necessary. The Newfie test will require you to individually load your cart under the supervision of the judges who will then inspect and ask you to individually move the cart forward in order to verify that the load is appropriate and the balance is correct. When all of the teams are loaded, the freight haul will commence by following the lead stewards. Newfie tests require two lead stewards and a steward assigned specifically to each team. If there are not enough stewards, the group size is reduced for the group exercise. The Rottie's, do not have a separate freight haul, so if you've already completed your maneuvering prior to the 'Group Down Stay,' your test is now complete for your particular class."

"What is the purpose of the stewards and do they have any judging responsibilities?" asked Mike.

"The stewards essentially work under the direction of the judges and they themselves are not considered judges, so they don't make any decisions regarding your performance. They are there to assist the teams. The lead steward is the moving target that the freight haul follows. This steward knows the course and sets the pace, stopping occasionally if the judges require that the group get closer together. The stewards nearer the carts assist in keeping other traffic clear of the carts, occasionally asking walkers or bike riders to wait while the teams move through an area. With a judge's permission, they also can

assist a team that gets fouled on an obstacle, or who has an equipment failure. Primarily these stewards are there to ensure the safety of your dogs, particularly if a cart is upset or the dog becomes injured.

"As to the freight haul itself, there are very few specific rules. The judges are looking for teamwork, willingness, and control. Freight haul courses are usually set up to get the teams a variety of different working surfaces, such as grass, asphalt, concrete, sand, pine needles, gravel, or whatever the locale provides. They also look for a few naturally-occurring obstacles, so don't be surprised to have to do some maneuvering around trees, onto or off of designated paths, and up and down hills if they are available.

"Ideally, you will hold whatever place in line you start with, but the teams will often naturally separate into faster and slower working dogs. If you have a faster dog, you may request permission from a judge to pass. You may do so only if permission is granted. Judges are looking for control here, so don't be surprised if permission is not granted, or if the judges tells you to wait for later in the freight haul or for some different terrain that is more suitable for allowing a pass without impacting the slower-working team. If the teams do separate, the judges may elect to split themselves and each will judge a part of the group, or they may request that the lead teams halt and wait for the slower teams to catch up, so be prepared to stop occasionally, and allow yourself plenty of following distance so that you have time to execute your halt without colliding into the team in front of you. While you will be primarily focused on your dog, remember to stay aware of the teams in front or behind you and be ready to act accordingly if someone else is having control issues.

"Berners haul for a minimum of one-half mile and have specific freight weight requirements. Novice will pull the cart plus twenty pounds for the load. Open will pull their weight rounded down to the nearest tem pounds, so a Berner weighing one hundred three pounds will pull one hundred pounds. Newfies haul for a mile and allow for a freight load weight of the handler's choosing varying from twenty-five to one hundred pounds for a wheeled apparatus and less for sleds, toboggans, or travois.

"For Berners, the exercise starts and concludes in the maneuvering ring. Once the final dog returns to the ring, the judge will call, 'Exercise Finished.' Bear in mind that this does not mean 'Test Finished,' as you are still being judged

until your dog has fully left the ring. If you are waiting for other teams behind you, leave plenty of room and find a nice spot to rest your dog until everyone is back. Then carefully leave the ring without hitting any other team, any obstacles, or the ring exit gate. You are not allowed to hit any obstacles or other carts during the freight haul, and your dog must not foul in the ring or while performing the group exercises.

"For Newfies, the freight haul starts wherever the 'Group Out-of-Sight' is located, which is typically not in the maneuvering ring. At the end of the Distance Freight Haul, the handler will wait in a designated area for the judges to observe unhitching the team from the cart. Unhitching occurs only when all the teams and both judges have reached the designated area, and is done in the order in which the dogs reach this area. Handlers, with permission from the judges, may elect to unload their cart prior to unhitching. Once unhitched, each team will be given an individual 'Exercise Finished' command, at which time your test is complete. The judges have some discretion to determine pass/fail for multiple minor bumps or even for a major collision. The judge will base their decision upon whether the team is out of control or demonstrating a lack of teamwork, in which case they will be failed. Finally, your dog may urinate once and may defecate once during the freight haul, but if they do defecate, you must clean up appropriately.

"Now that you have heard everything explained, let's give this a try. We'll get harnessed and hitched and we'll just randomly move through the park, playing follow-the-leader. I'll go first and set the course, so you get some practice following. Once we turn around and are heading for home, ask for permission to pass, I'll halt and let you go by, and then I'll follow you back."

Preparing for a Test

"I know your original idea for drafting was 'Just a Walk in the Park,' and I must say, I've really enjoyed watching your progress. Watching you work with Shogun and the difference from where you started to now is pretty amazing. In just a few short weeks, you've worked your way through every exercise I could throw at you. I'll bet that just following these foot paths through the park is feeling pretty simple."

"I have a feeling I know where this is going," said Mike. "I have a feeling you're about to ask if I'm ready to give competition a try."

"It is the logical next step, and since we happen to live in an area where the regional club puts on tests twice a year, it won't require much travel, and the cost of entry is pretty minor – usually in the $35 to $40 range. I won't put any pressure on you, although I think you're ready to compete and could probably pass at this point. If you do plan to send in an entry, I've got a few more things for you to keep in mind.

"First of all, consider everything I've taught you as the minimum criteria for being able to participate in a test. The test itself is made up of exercises meant to challenge you by simulating actual working conditions you would encounter as you draft with your dog. However, I believe that many handlers view the draft test as the most difficult thing they ever expect their dog to work through, and unfortunately, that's how they practice. You never want to use a test as an opportunity to see what your dog can really do. You should already know that going in. You'll never be nervous that your dog won't be able to complete an

exercise if you already know that they are capable of the exercise and far more.

"When I train my dogs, I always work them over time up to conditions far worse than anything I ever expect to encounter during a draft test. I work them up to freight loads greater than what they will pull for the test. I work them for distances far longer than the freight haul. I work hills far bigger than any reasonable judge would ever include in a test. I back them for many feet beyond the four-foot requirement. I get them stuck in impossibly tight situations or stall them in ruts and make them pivot turn, back, or pull their way out of it. I train in snow and rain and soggy ground and I try for both shade and sunny conditions. In short, the test becomes one of the easier sets of exercises they are ever expected to perform.

"Many of the people I have seen who have difficulties with the test appear to be working beyond the capabilities of their dogs because for many of them, the level of difficulty of the test is equal to or often above what they have practiced, or above what they believe the capabilities of their dogs to be. When they ask their dogs for the little extra they need to get them out of a tough spot or through a difficult freight haul, they don't know whether the dog can or will be able to deliver. If you practice to a higher level of difficulty before you ever attend a test, you not only know your dog can deliver, you should also know how to ask for the extra you need from them and you can expect to get it. Obviously, there will always be exceptions for elderly dogs or dogs with various medical conditions as to how much extra practice stress is appropriate, but these should be the exceptions and not the rule.

"I believe that anyone conducting workshops or practice sessions, or offering advice to handlers should standardize on the message that the skills required in order to successfully complete our tests represent a minimum expectation of drafting capabilities. Training to simply meet minimum expectations should not be encouraged. Training to exceed minimum expectations should be strongly recommended."

"So how do you recommend we proceed with increasing the level of difficulty?" asked Mike.

"Well, you can increase everything slowly over a few sessions, or you can increase until you feel yourself working at the edge of Shogun's capabilities,

and then you can back off just a bit. Remember to always end any exercise on a good note, so if this means stepping back a few notches on any given day, so be it. If you do decide to enter a BMDCA draft test, you will be starting in Novice class, so you will be handling on-leash, performing the Basic Control and Recall, backing one foot, working through a three-minute in-sight stay, and carrying twenty pounds in your cart.

"I'd start increasing the difficulty by practicing far more elaborate heeling patterns, including backing-up while not harnessed, and I'd increase the time and distance for the Recall exercise including a longer 'Wait' before you call him, and a distance far beyond forty feet. Practice this exercise just using your hand signal recall as well, just in case it gets noisy and Shogun can't hear you.

"My next suggestion would be between now and the test, that you work yourself up to at least the skills required for the Open class. This means you should be confident to work off-leash, you should be able to back at least four feet, you can perform the stay as an out-of-sight exercise with you being gone for four to five minutes, and you can start working your way up to a freight load of his weight or beyond for a distance of anywhere from three-quarters to a full mile.

"If you do these things, not only will you be very confident in your Novice class capabilities, but if you enter as Novice for both days of a two-day test, you will have the option of moving up to Open class on the second day, assuming you pass on the first. Depending upon how well your practice sessions progress and if you want to consider the possibility of a move up, the only stipulation here is that when you send in your entry, you will need to include a weight certificate signed by a Veterinarian so that the Secretary knows how much weight you will be required to pull for Open. Also check you calendar carefully since the weight certificate can be dated no earlier than sixty days from the date of the test."

"Well, that certainly ups the ante for training sessions, but I've already been following your advice and trying a few of these suggestions on my own." Said Mike. "Frankly, I always thought that twenty pounds was really not very much weight, but if I can work him up over a hundred pounds, that would be pretty impressive."

"Not to mention that if you draft with that much weight, you can give Shogun a far greater workout in a far shorter walk than you usually do."

"I've never seen a test before, what else do I need to know?"

"If you have the opportunity to see a test before you enter, this will make you more familiar with the process, but if not, there are a few things to keep in mind. Read the premium carefully and make sure you submit your entries according to the instructions. The forms can be a little tricky the first couple of times, especially if you are planning more than one entry on a given day. Make sure you send the correct entry fee to the correct address. If the club offers meals for purchase, most will ask you to send a separate check for the food, occasionally to a different address than the Secretary. Sometimes food, including a continental breakfast is included or available for a donation to the club. If not, make sure you pack food for yourself and for your dog.

"Even if you are only entering once, be prepared to be on site all day. Check in is usually pretty early in the morning. You will need to pick up your entry packet from the Secretary or if the club is using self check-in you will probably have been contacted by the Secretary with your entry number so you can find your packet hanging in a pre-assigned location where you will place your cart and draft equipment. Check in is followed by the equipment check.

"You do not necessarily need to be present at the equipment check, although I would certainly recommend it for the first few times, and you don't need to have your dog at equipment check. However, you do need your cart completely set up with your entry number attached, as well as your harness, traces, leash, and collar, as well as your freight load weights and any attaching mechanism including a weight insert or bungie cords. Once your cart is inspected and measured for width for setting the Narrows correctly, you will not be able to make modifications to your equipment without approval from a judge, so make sure that everything is firmly fastened and that your tires are properly inflated before the equipment check begins. Since it can get confusing shuttling a leash and collar to and from your dog for inspection, I'd recommend that you bring one set that you only use only for drafting and Shogun's normal collar and leash for getting him from the car to your set-up and for walking him around the grounds during the day. I usually switch to the drafting leash and collar just before I get ready to go into the ring.

"While you are not allowed to train on the site of the test, you can elect to harness and hitch your dog for the purpose of drafting the equipment to or from the equipment check. This is considered a practical application of draft work, so it is permitted."

"What do you mean by 'set-up'?" asked Mike.

"Your set-up is pretty much everything else you're going to need for a day of competition. Like most other dog events, you'll spend a lot of time waiting around until it's your turn to participate. Pass or fail, once you've finished, it's considered good sportsmanship to cheer on the other competitors and wait for the awards ceremony at the end of the test. This means you're probably going to spend a good part of the day at the test site, so you and your dog may as well be comfortable.

"Some people will choose to use their car as their set-up, but often parking is not directly adjacent to the ring. Some parks offer pavilions that you can use, and people will set-up there, primarily for the shade. Many people will bring pop-up canopies and set-up somewhat near the ring so they can watch the proceedings. If you have any doubt about possible conflicts with ring entrances or exits or freight haul routes, ask a judge or a steward before you start unloading your equipment.

"As to what else to bring, you will probably want a chair for yourself, a crate or x-pen for your dog, and water for your dog. You might consider a small toolkit with the necessary wrenches to assemble, disassemble, and adjust your cart, plus spare inner tubes, and a bicycle pump. You can bring a cooler with anything else you want to eat or drink, and many people will bring treats for your dog, but remember that you cannot use these or bring them with you during any portion of the competition, so get in the habit of never putting these in your pocket so you don't have to worry about forgetting them. Some people bring tarps to place on the ground or over their crates or x-pens so they don't have to move them around as the sun changes its angle throughout the day. With the exception of lightning, you will probably be competing in just about any other weather, so make sure you have rain gear and extra layers available if it is going to be wet or cold."

"Well all of that makes sense. It sounds like you're saying that we're going to be

pretty much sitting around for most of the day."

"You'll see handlers who have multiple entries across multiple classes, so they're up and down a lot, but for the most part, you will be sitting around. After the equipment check, you will have the opportunity to participate in the walkthrough of the maneuvering and freight haul courses. Berner tests do not allow your dogs to accompany you on the walkthroughs, but Newfie tests do, and the Rottie rules don't specify. I prefer to leave my dogs crated during the walkthroughs regardless of the test. After the walkthroughs, the test will begin for the first dog typically five to fifteen minutes later.

"Unless you're the first dog in the ring, which is usually an Open dog by the way, then you should have plenty of time to get your dog ready to go. Remember that you are going to be trying to strike a balance between a dog that is calm and relaxed, and one that has the energy and interest in working with you. Much like everything else we've talked about related to drafting, you are going to have to experiment and see what works best for you and your dog. Some dogs are content to sleep in their crate, and others will whine and howl, especially if you are out of sight. You may need to keep your dog out and leashed if they absolutely have to be with you every minute, but this can get very tiring for both the dog and the handler.

"Also, give some thought to your feeding regimen. I prefer not to draft my dogs on a full stomach, but they will also need energy to get through the test. I usually give my dogs about a half of their normal breakfast, especially if they are going to be in the ring early in the day. If they are only entered in the afternoon, then a full breakfast is fine. Remember that they can't potty in the ring or on the freight haul, so as soon as you get them to the site, you'll want to start making sure they have the opportunity to go several times before they get into the ring. Few things are more discouraging than failing an otherwise perfect performance because your dog suddenly had to go while on the freight haul. You will have some time between your ring performance and your group exercises, so take that opportunity to get them to potty again if necessary.

"Above all else, remember that this really is 'Just a Walk in the Park.' This is an event where you and your dog get to spend the entire day together doing something that is hopefully fun and exciting for both of you. Try to remain upbeat and encouraging to your dog, no matter what mistake you make,

remembering that there are no bad dogs, only bad handlers! Regardless of what happens, before, during, or after the test, you and your dog are going home together, hopefully with some fond memories of a great day at the park. And you might even get to bring home a ribbon or two."

So you've put in all the effort, the endless practice sessions and you've competed and finally passed your first draft test. Good for you! You get to bring home the spoils – ribbons, and trophies, and prizes, and photographs to show all of your friends.

Other than the fun of seeing you excited and happy, what does your dog get after the competition is over? You may get some dog treats as ring favors or prizes, and you can feel free to treat away. Your dog is certainly not going to refuse.

Perhaps a pat on the head and a 'job well done?' In truth, that's really what your dog wants most. Recognition that they've done something to please you, and you will seldom get any arguments from them telling you otherwise.

I prefer a bit of a celebration ritual that occurs once we get home. When my dogs pass a draft test, they get... steak! That's right, steak! This is typically not going to be filet mignon or prime rib, but I've never had any of them refuse a share of five pounds of chuck steak, cubed and sprinkled with a little garlic powder. I place their bowls down and this is gone in seconds. If any one passes, they all get to share.

Now I have no idea if this proves to be motivational to them in any way, nor do I know enough about canine psychology to know whether they can equate the cause and effect relationship of one of them passing a draft test with all of them sharing a steak dinner that night. All I know is that the ritual seems to make them very happy. Later, when I see them curled up or stretched out on the floor, with full bellies and what I can only describe as a smile on their faces, I'm truly happy too.

Over the course of my drafting career, I've been fortunate to have some success, and in turn I've spent a good deal of money purchasing steaks for my dogs. I recall one particularly successful weekend at the park that kept them eating steak dinners every night for a week. And you know what? It's been worth every penny.

Alphabet Soup and Goodie Bags

"Other than the enjoyment of having a 'Just a Walk in the Park' well-trained dog, what else do you get out of participating in drafting?" asked Mike.

"Many people will pursue drafting as an activity for nothing more than the desire to do something fun with their dogs. For others, they will wish to participate in parades, giving rides to children, or doing practical drafting such as hauling logs or fulfilling other utility purposes around their home or farm. However, if you have the loftier goal of drafting for the associated titles, and you are especially fond of the title abbreviations that can be included with your dog's registered name, than drafting offers a literal smorgasbord of letters you can append. I like to call it the pursuit of Alphabet Soup. And while no one is ever going to get rich drafting, most clubs offer a nice array of prizes and ribbons to go along with your qualifying performances.

"The Bernese Mountain Dog Club of America offers the widest array of titles. For individual dogs you must start by competing for your Novice Draft Dog (NDD) title, which is an on-lead test. Once your dog has earned that title, you can pursue their Draft Dog (DD) title, which is off lead, and has a higher degree of difficulty, or you can pursue their Brace Novice Draft Dog (BNDD), which is identical to the NDD, except it features two dogs side-by-side pulling the cart. Finally, once your dog has earned a DD and a BNDD, you can pursue their Brace Draft Dog (BDD) title, which is identical to the DD except with a two dogs instead of an individual dog.

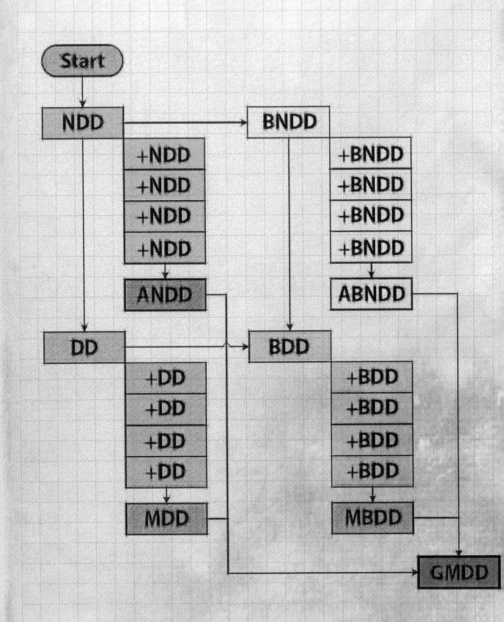

"If that's still not enough titles for you, the rules also allow for repetitive versions of each of the four base titles. If you qualify for a NDD title five times under a total of at least seven different judges, your dog will earn their Advanced Novice Draft Dog (ANDD) title. Similarly, with five individual DD titles under at least seven judges, your dog earns their Master Draft Dog (MDD) title. The same thing applies to the brace titles – five BNDD titles under seven judges earns your dog their Advanced Brace Novice Draft Dog (ABNDD) and five BDD titles under seven judges earns you dog their Master Brace Draft Dog title."

"If you are willing to put in the time and the effort to earn all four of the advanced and master titles, you complete what used to be called the 'Clean Sweep' of titles. Now, this has been renamed with a far simpler and more elegant club award – Grand Master Draft Dog (GMDD). As you might imagine, Master Brace Draft Dog is pretty rare in and of itself, mostly due to the complexity of having two draft dogs in their prime able to practice and compete together and pull the necessary freight load. Grand Master Draft Dog is also exceptionally rare with only twenty-two total club awards having been earned through the middle of the 2015 calendar year."

"What get's most people participating in draft tests in the first place?" asked Mike.

"Many people competing for BMDCA titles start with the goal of earning their NDD title in order to complete their Versatility Dog (VD) special award which consists of a confirmation title; a working title in obedience, agility, tracking or herding; and a draft title. Other people will set their goal of earning one each of the available titles in the various classes. More recently, people draft as one of their primary working goals, and they will target completing advanced and/or master titles in one or more classes.

"Available titles formerly included just NDD, DD, BNDD, and BDD. At that time it was common to omit the novice titles on the dog's registered name once the open titles were earned. So Fido, NDD would become Fido, DD for example, and Fido DD, BNDD would become Fido DD, BDD.

"Since the rules update in 2008 that added the advanced and master titles, it is now common for people to list up to all four classes as part of the dog's registered name as they work through their title progression. Now Fido NDD, often becomes Fido NDD, DD, BNDD, BDD on his way to Fido ANDD, MDD, BNDD, BDD, and eventually Fido ANDD, MDD, ABNDD, MBDD. As I said before, this is more than enough title letters for even the most diligent collector, and for those who have completed everything, we can now proudly trade all of that in and say Fido, GMDD.

"Once you have experience working through the title progression, if your desire is to work towards a GMDD club award as quickly as possible, then you can try to incorporate the following tips. First, train your dog for both novice and open at the same time. You must initially enter the NDD class, but with the advent of two or more day tests back-to-back, you can enter NDD on each of the test days.

"Upon qualifying for your NDD, you can 'move up' in class to DD the next day, assuming you and your dog are ready to do so, and you have included your dog's open weight certificate as part of your entry. In this way, in a single weekend, you could earn both the NDD and DD titles. This means that you can enter in both NDD and DD classes on each day of your next test, which allows you to progress much more quickly.

"Next, train your dogs for both novice brace and open brace at the same time. Once you have earned your NDD, at your second test, enter in both DD and NBDD both days, plus NDD if you are so inclined and confident that your dog has the stamina to complete more than once. Remember, entering these three classes will only require a single freight haul with a full open dog weight load, so many dogs may be capable of two or three entries in a single testing day.

"If you pass BNDD and have already passed DD or can pass DD the same day, then you can 'move up' in class to BDD the next day, assuming you and your dogs are ready to do so, and you have included your dogs' open weight certificates as part of your entry.

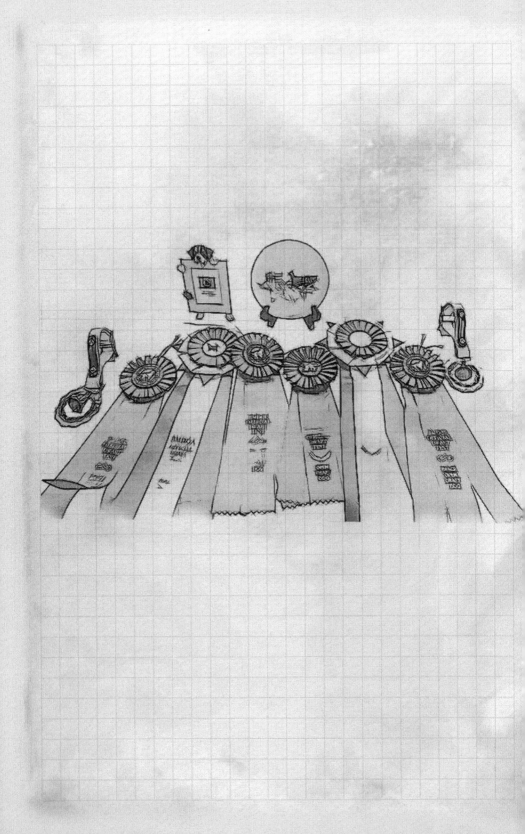

"If you progress through only one new class each time you test, it will take you at least four test weekends to qualify for all four classes, and if your club only offers a single test each year and you aren't inclined to drive to another club's test, this process can easily run into several years. Ideally the approach I've described gets you qualified for all four classes by the end of your second test weekend, in which case you have the maximum flexibility to enter any and all classes you want in all subsequent tests.

"If your goal is to truly pursue a GMDD, I suggest you work 'backwards' by completing advanced and master brace titles before completing your individual advanced and master titles. Competing in brace can often be a tricky business as you are dependent upon the availability and willingness of two dogs instead of one. Often, handlers must rely on someone else's dog to complete their brace team, but even if you own both of the dogs, something can often happen where you need to pull one of the dogs for any variety of reasons.

"Practice can become more complicated and you will find yourself dealing with more equipment and heavier weight loads, which can often make travelling logistics more difficult as well. Unfortunately, once submitted, a brace entry cannot be changed, so even if there is another dog available, you would not be able to make this substitution on the day of the test.

"Once you are qualified for brace competition, focus your efforts on brace, and then pick up additional individual entries as bonuses, subject to how comfortable you are competing with your dog more than once per day. Once you have your advanced and/or master brace titles, then you can concentrate on picking you any remaining individual titles knowing that the logistics to do so will be less complicated.

"BMDCA qualifiers are awarded a certificate for each new title earned. Advanced and Master titles also grant the qualifier a page in the BMDCA yearbook, and with the exception of the ANDD, earn the qualifier a plaque at the National Specialty Show Awards Banquet. Host clubs for tests typically award ribbons, prizes, or a combination of both. Ring favors may also be given."

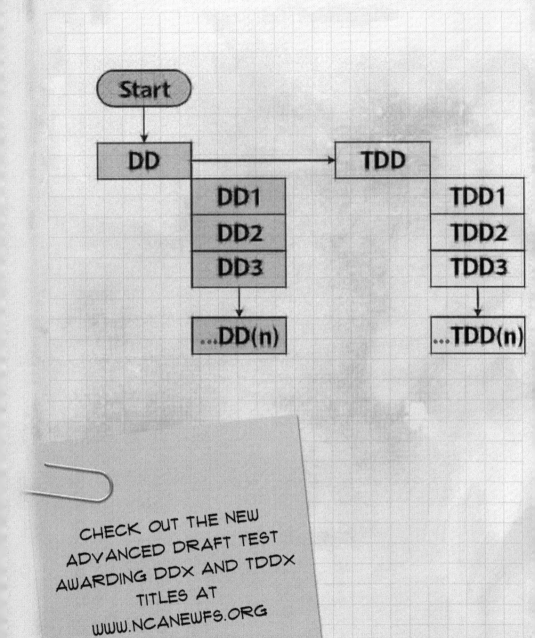

"The Newfoundland Club of America offers a Draft Dog (DD) title for their off lead test. You can then perform a Draft Dog Requalification at a subsequent test as many times as you like, earning a new number after the title. For example a DD1 has re-qualified one time.

"For teams of two or more dogs, your dog can earn a Team Draft Dog (TDD) title, and can then earn a Team Draft Dog Requalification, for example a TDD2 has re-qualified two times.

"All dogs must enter competition at the DD-level. Dogs having qualified as DD can them enter at the TDD-level.

"NCA tests award prizes to qualifiers at the discretion of the host club. Ring favors may also be given."

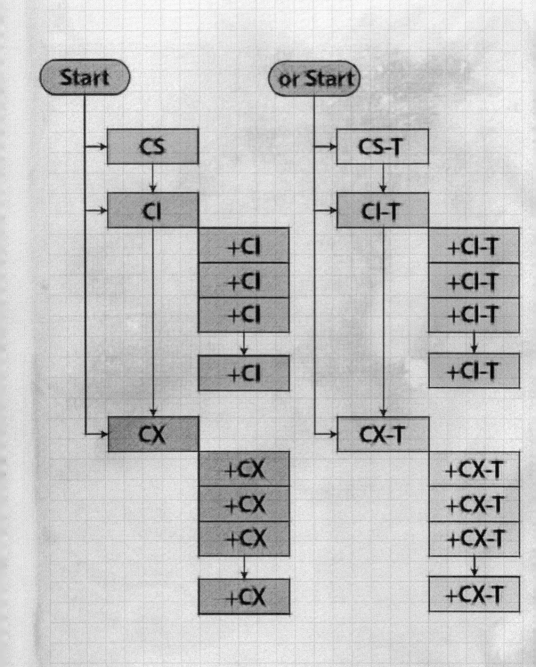

"The American Rottweiler Club offers three levels for individual dogs, including the Carting Started (CS) title for their on lead test, the Carting Intermediate (CI) title for their off lead test, and the Carting Excellent (CX) title for their driving test where the dog pulls their handler in a Sulky-style cart.

"Similar titles are awarded for teams: the Carting Started Team (CS-T) title, the Carting Intermediate Team (CI-T) title and the Carting Excellent Team (CX-T) title. Dogs can enter at any level. Once a dog has qualified for their CS title, they must go to either the CI or CX-level. A CI dog can continue at the CI-level or can go on to CX -level. A CX dog can continue competing at the CX-level.

"ARC qualifiers receive ribbons for qualifying scores, as well as first through fourth place in each division, as well as a "High in Test" ribbon to the overall high score. The host club also has the option to award a "Reserve High in Test" ribbon as well. The host club may also award prizes at their discretion. Ring favors may be given.

"So what is the ultimate achievement for the alphabet collector? Perhaps it would be Fido, ANDD, MDD, ABNDD, MBDD, DD4, TDD4, CX, CX-T.

So many tests, so little time…"

"It is not the will to win that matters - everyone has that.
It's the will to prepare to win that matters."

~ Paul "Bear" Bryant

Made in the USA
Middletown, DE
31 July 2019